"*The Missionary Call* by Dr. David Sills is a valuable, objective, and comprehensive review of this subject. Distorted perceptions and misunderstandings regarding who is called and what consists of a call to missions abound, but Dr. Sills deals with every perspective from a biblical and practical consideration. This book will be a valuable contribution to the church mobilizing God's people to be obedient to our Great Commission task."

Jerry Rankin
President, International Mission Board

"Dr. Sills leads his readers through a methodical evaluation of the complexities of a missionary calling without being formulaic or unnecessarily mysterious. This book should be in the tool kit of anyone exploring a calling to cross-cultural ministry. I will recommend it to all of Wycliffe's candidates."

Bob Creson
President, Wycliffe Bible Translators

"Dr. Sills has done an excellent work in removing the mystery of God's call on our lives. If you're serious about investing your life in what is important to God then this is a must read to ground you in the overarching purpose of God and how He planned on you fitting into that! Oh, and if you're not serious, then this is definitely the book for you!"

Larry Brown
Chairman/CEO, New Tribes Mission

"If you are wondering about the missionary call, this book will be a life saver for you. David Sills thoroughly explores the subject and gives information that the ordinary person feeling called would not know. His is not a cut-and-dried answer, and he leaves the final answer to the leading to the mysterious working of God's Spirit. This will become a classic book dealing with the missionary call."

Avery Willis
Executive Director, International Orality Network

D0089481

"There is a crying need today for men and women who are willing to give their lives to the great cause of proclaiming the Gospel to the nations. Dr. David Sills offers practical help in thinking through the call to missions—from discerning whether God has called you to missions to determining how and where you should serve. A scholarly missiologist with hands-on missionary experience, Dr. Sills provides sound pastoral advice to Christians wondering if God might be calling them to spend their lives as missionaries in the service of the Gospel. I am absolutely confident that this book will make a big difference in many lives."

> R. Albert Mohler, Jr.
> President, The Southern Baptist Theological Seminary

"*The Missionary Call* is a superb work that is certain to become a valuable tool for all Great Commission Christians. It is filled with biblical and practical wisdom. I was amazed that David covered so much and did it so well in so few pages. This a fine gift to the body of Christ. I know the students at our seminary and college will be reading it!"

> Danny Akin
> President, Southeastern Baptist Theological Seminary

"David Sills has addressed the single, burning issue in this, the greatest era of mission expansion in the history of the Christian Church. *The Missionary Call* presents a powerful, scripturally sound and convincing response for anyone considering a vocation in missions. I would urge every pastor and church missions leader to keep multiple copies of this book on hand as a reliable resource for anyone considering the call to missions."

> Tom Elliff
> Senior Vice President for Spiritual Nurture &
> Church Relations, International Mission Board

"The question of the 'missionary call' has been debated, dissected, analyzed and written about for generations. Dr. Sills has produced refreshingly new insights into an old topic. His breadth of scholarship covers the biblical, historical, spiritual, contemporary, and pragmatic aspects of this vital topic in delightfully readable fashion. This is the finest single book on this fascinating topic that I have ever read. I heartily recommend it for students, pastors, professors, missionaries, and every follower of Jesus Christ."

David M. Howard
Former President, Latin America Mission
Former International Director of the
    World Evangelical Fellowship
Former Missions Director of IVCF and
    Director of URBANA 73 and 76

"Dr. Sills provides a solid and well-grounded exploration of the missionary call. He offers significant help in clarifying the issues for those who struggle with whether God is calling them into missionary service and a great resource for those who teach about the call as it relates to missionary life."

Scott Moreau
Professor of Missions & Intercultural Studies,
    Wheaton College
Editor, Evangelical Missions Quarterly

"No aspect of missions is more bogged down with extra-biblical baggage than 'the missionary call.' Is not the clear command of Christ 'to go' enough to set you on your way to unreached regions? You can't go wrong by trying to go. Be aggressive to go. The Lord will direct your moving feet. Dr. Sills presents this and other popular views on how a person may be called into mission. I strongly recommend this practical book that cuts through much of the confusion of the missionary call."

David Sitton
President, To Every Tribe Ministries

"At last! Here is a book on a fundamental issue of missions that is at once truly readable, theologically balanced, biblically grounded, and practically oriented. David Sills draws upon his own experience on the field and in the classroom, the salient research of other scholars, and the wise reflection of a heart given over to the purpose for which his Lord left the palaces of heaven to dwell among a lost humanity. Engagingly written and immensely practical, Sills' book addresses with winsomeness and clarity the often bewildering questions that each of us who would follow Jesus today must face regarding our place in the missionary task. This book is a 'must read' for introductory courses on missions, for missionaries already on the field and those considering missionary service, for mission agency staff, and for pastors, missions committees, and church members alike. Highly recommended!"

> Samuel Larsen
> Samuel Patterson Professor of Missions and Evangelism,
> Reformed Theological Seminary

"Can a book be brief and thorough? Clear and scholarly? Simple and profound? Practical and heartwarming? This one is. It will be a great help to many."

> Joe Martin
> Chair of the Biblical Studies and Ministries Department,
> Belhaven College

"I've been involved in 'missions in other countries' for over forty years, and Dr. Sills, in *The Missionary Call*, gives me increased excitement concerning how this generation will respond to the missionary call placed on their lives. I would like for every Christian to read this book. God does call all of us to be missionaries, some to go and some to stay. Dr. Sills has given us an exciting and excellent tool to use, along with His Word, to determine which it is that the Lord is commanding us to do. Nothing is more exciting than being faithful to the call that He places on your life!"

> Sammy Simpson
> President, Global Outreach

"There is a broad spectrum of opinions concerning the definition and even existence of such a concept as the 'missionary call.' Dr. Sills scans the pages of Scripture and the landscape of the last three centuries of missiological thought and provides the reader with an informative and practical presentation of this key issue in cross-cultural disciple making."

Timothy R. Sisk
Professor & Chair, Department of World Missions & Evangelism, Moody Bible Institute

"From advice for beginners—know God, and know His Word—to advice for those seriously committed to such a career—choose the right mission agency for you, and get to know the missionary team you will be working with—anyone interested in the details of a personal, missionary call will find much food for thought."

David Ross
President, Graduate Institute of Applied Linguistics

THE
MISSIONARY
CALL

THE
MISSIONARY
CALL

FIND YOUR PLACE IN GOD'S
PLAN *for the* WORLD

M. DAVID SILLS

MOODY PUBLISHERS
CHICAGO

Editor: Christopher Reese
Interior Design: Ragont Design
Cover Design: Brand Navigation (www.brandnavigation.com)
Cover Image: iStock (www.istockphoto.com)

Library of Congress Cataloging-in-Publication Data

Sills, M. David (Michael David)
The missionary call : find your place in God's plan for the world / M. David Sills.
    p. cm.
Includes bibliographical references and index.
ISBN-13: 978-0-8024-5028-9
ISBN-10: 0-8024-5028-8
1. Missionaries--Appointment, call, and election. I. Title.
BV2063.S54 2008
266--dc22
                              2008010942

We hope you enjoy this book from Moody Publishers. Our goal is to provide high-quality, thought-provoking books and products that connect truth to your real needs and challenges. For more information on other books and products written and produced from a biblical perspective, go to www.moodypublishers.com or write to:

Moody Publishers
820 N. LaSalle Boulevard
Chicago, IL 60610

7 9 10 8 6

Printed in the United States of America

To Mary, my bride and best friend for thirty years,
To Christopher, my firstborn son and friend,
And to Molly, Daddy's girl and joy.

Under God, and by His grace,
the three of you have walked with me in our
missionary call through many years
and several countries.
The best is yet to come!
I love you and thank God for you every day.

CONTENTS

FOREWORD

"ARE YOU STEVE SAINT?" the man asked me. "Are you the son of the famous missionary who was martyred with four others down in South America?"

I acknowledged that I was Nate Saint's son. "Oh, and where are you a missionary?" I did not know what to say. I wasn't a missionary, I was a businessman. My wife and I were raising our four children to be God followers. We were active in our local Christian church where we served as leaders of a growing youth group that met in our home. We were living below our means so we could help support others to go to the "ends of the earth." And I felt sure that I was right where God wanted me, confident that Ginny and I were doing what God had called us to do.

When I told my inquisitor that I was not, in fact, a missionary but a businessman, he looked puzzled. Then, as my answer sunk in, he answered with obvious disappointment, "Oh, I'm so sorry."

Now, years later, people just like that man come up to me on a regular basis and ask me if I am Nate Saint's son. Then they tell me that they have heard that I am a missionary working with the very people who killed my dad.

A look of wonder comes over them, and they say things like, "Oh, we're so proud of you."

Why so proud now and so disappointed then?

I believe it is that many of us have misunderstood that there is only one priority in serving God. We are to be His faithful servants and good stewards of His mysteries (1 Corinthians 4:1). We are supposed to obey.

Ah, but there comes the rub. What if we don't know God's plan for our lives? I can tell you what has worked for me. Pray a lot, wait expectantly for God to answer, and seek wise counsel from those who have learned to understand how God shows us His plan for our lives.

Thank you, David, for taking the time to put down on paper what you have learned from study and personal experience about finding God's will for our lives.

I believe it was a U.S. president who said, "There is no greater blessing in life than to have something to do that is worth doing and the ability to do it." After almost six decades of life experience I would modify that statement a bit. I would say, "There is no greater blessing in life than to know that we are right in the middle of the trail God has marked for our lives and to know that He is providing the strength and endurance to play our part in His plan for the World."

Until my only daughter died suddenly and unexpectedly at twenty years of age—in the middle of a long-anticipated party we were having to welcome her home after a year of traveling with a Christian music group—I thought that the worst thing that could happen in life was people going into a Christless eternity without ever hearing that the Creator of the universe loved them and had a plan for their lives.

Now I know something even worse. The real, compassionate, and all-loving heavenly Father of the cosmos is losing children every day. I believe that I will spend eternity with my precious daughter. I believe God promises that in His Word. But that same Word suggests that His children, the ones dying without being reconciled to Him, will be separated from Him forever.

Not everyone is called to be a missionary. But missions is for everyone. As a father with a deeply wounded heart, I believe I can say with confidence that nothing can be more dear to God's heart than telling His children who don't know it that He loves them and wants them to live with Him forever.

I pray you will find God's mission for your life in His plan for the world.

If you haven't found it yet, then I suggest you just keep on reading. If you think you have found your place in God's plan, I suggest you keep reading and make sure.

STEVE SAINT
Founder, I-Tec

INTRODUCTION

CHRISTIANS EVERYWHERE and of all ages recognize God's heartbeat to take the gospel to the nations and wrestle with the implications of the Great Commission in their own lives. Many ask how they can know for sure that God is calling them to missions. But the practical concerns inherent in discerning God's will about whether to join Him in missionary service usually throw us into a crisis because of the comfort-zone-exploding ramifications of surrendering to that call. Christians direct questions about their general understanding of the call and the implications of such a vocation to college and seminary professors, pastors, mission agencies, missionaries, and friends. They ask what exactly constitutes a missionary call, how detailed it must be, and how God communicates such a call to His children. Many wonder whether a specific and personal call is necessary since it seems to them that all Christians are called and the obedient respond. Even if they are certain of a personal call to missions, they are still left with the dilemma of discovering the elusive details of where, when, how, and with whom the calling is to be fulfilled. Some who believe they are called to missions struggle with how they can follow God's calling when their spouse does not yet feel called. Confusion abounds for most believers about the missionary call.

Very few books address the missionary call as it practically applies to people in the twenty-first century. Issues such as terrorism, globalization, urbanization, and pluralism have changed the missions landscape. While some mission agencies have responded to these challenges with innovations such as creative-access platforms to provide access and protection in dangerous places, others are openly calling for missionary martyrs. Some speakers and missions literature say that all are called to go while others say that no one should go without a specific calling. Discernment can be difficult under the best of circumstances and these complications just make knowing and doing the will of the Lord seem even more difficult.

A misunderstanding of the missionary call, who receives it, and how it comes to people has probably kept more people from going to the mission field than any other reason. Perhaps you are one of the many young people anxiously wondering whether God is calling you to missions. Or maybe you are one of the hundreds of thousands of faithful church members approaching middle age with kids who are now in college or married with families of their own. You want to finish your life well and would love to serve on the mission field with your remaining years. Christians just like you, all around the globe, also struggle with the question: Is God calling me to missions? It is not an easy question to answer and the life-changing consequences that could follow make it all the more important.

Young believers often suffer the paralysis of analysis while seeking to know God's will for missions in their lives. Confronted with a host of opportunities and the sincere desire to serve God, they desperately want to know what God wants them to do. J. Herbert Kane, former missionary and missions professor at Trinity Evangelical Divinity School, wrote, "No aspect of the Christian mission is more puzzling than this problem of a call. It is the biggest hang-up that young people have as they face the claims of the mission field."[1] Kane believed that the idea of the missionary call is misunderstood and problematic. Nonetheless, missions history, literature, experience, and preaching refer to it regularly and seem to assume both an understanding of the missionary call and the assurance of it to be a faithful, effective missionary.

Sometimes the angst begins after attending a missions rally like Urbana, hearing a missionary speaker at church, going on a mission trip, or taking a missions class. Faced with the overwhelming physical and spiritual needs throughout the developing majority of the world, it is easy to feel guilty for having the many blessings we enjoy. We hear rousing missions slogans from speakers who tell us that God has already called and it falls to us only to obey or disobey. While we are seeking God's direction, we hear other speakers telling us not to go without a definite missionary call. Indeed, some mission agencies will not allow candidates to go unless both husband and wife can articulate a clear and definite missionary call to the field. Where does one go to resolve these issues?

God's Word speaks to us about missions from beginning to end. Indeed, biblical scholars like Christopher J. H. Wright[2] and missiologists like Ralph D. Winter[3] point out the inadequacy of the term "biblical basis of missions" and prefer to speak of the missional basis of the Bible. This perspective points out that the reason God revealed Himself to us in His Word was that we might know Him and make Him known. God has commanded us to go to the nations and proclaim His glory until they do too. So, is this to say that all Christians are missionaries?

Years ago, I heard a very broad definition of a missionary: A missionary is someone who never gets used to the sound of pagan footsteps on their way to a Christless eternity. Many Christian hearts resonate with this definition. They feel the weight of the missionary task that remains and want their lives to impact the vast areas of lostness in the world. These same Christians then begin to wonder whether this burden for the nations is a missionary call. They are profoundly motivated to rescue the perishing when they remember that millions around the world are one breath away from an eternity separated from Christ; they long to take them the gospel.

A desire for obedience to the clear commission from Christ to His followers motivates others. Missions speakers often urge us to make Christ's last command our first concern. Mindful of the many biblical passages represented by Luke 6:46, "Why do you call me 'Lord, Lord,' and not do what I tell you?" these believers set their hearts to be obedient. Is this desire to obey the same as the missionary call? Is the Great Commission all that is necessary for a missionary call to set out for the mission field?

Making friends with internationals and traveling around the world open us up to the greater world around us. Every person's default setting of ethnocentrism[4] makes them think that their culture is the center of the universe and judge all other cultures as inferior in comparison. The Kikuyu of Kenya have a proverb, "The man who has never traveled thinks his mother is the best cook," that illustrates this naïve perspective. The prejudice and stereotypes that we have learned in our home cultures are quickly broken down when we make friends with those in other cultures and travel to their countries. Mark Twain said, "Travel is fatal to prejudice, bigotry, and narrow-mindedness, and many of our people need it sorely on these accounts. Broad, wholesome, charitable views of men and things cannot be acquired by vegetating in one little corner of the earth all one's lifetime."[5] International exposure also teaches us about the needs and opportunities awaiting us around the world. As Ralph D. Winter observes, "God cannot lead you on the basis of facts you do not have."[6] Developing international friendships and traveling the world are often beginning points of the missionary call.

In the journey to discern whether God has placed a missionary call on our lives, we often encounter a maze of paths to follow.

Conflicting opinions and exhortations often leave us with more questions than answers. In this book we will see what God's Word teaches about the missionary call, examine biblical and historical examples of God's call, and learn how to bring this knowledge to bear on personal experience. We will consider these issues and more as we take a journey together to understand the missionary call and how it applies to each of our lives.

PART 1

WHAT IS THE
MISSIONARY CALL?

UNDERSTANDING THE MISSIONARY CALL

"NOW THAT GOD HAS called you to missions . . ." Wait a minute! What exactly does "the missionary call" mean? The vast majority of articles and books that address the missionary call begin with an assumption that you know you have received a call and seek to help you take the next step. Many sermons, missions books, and youth group challenges use the term frequently, but without explaining it. To make matters worse, they all seem to have widely differing understandings of what "the call" actually is. The Bible speaks of a call to salvation, calls to serve the Lord, and calls to some specific service. The Bible also gives examples of specific guidance in understanding where and when people are to express their calling, but many confuse this guidance with the call itself. How then should we understand the missionary call?

Many missionaries can testify that they knew when the Lord saved them that it was for some particular service. I was not sure what the Lord would do with my life when He saved me, but I clearly remember thinking that I had wasted many years of my life. I wanted the rest of them to count in a sacrificial way for Christ's glory and the advance of His kingdom. I considered continuing as a businessman, being as faithful in the local church as possible, and serving in my free time. However, mission trips began to change my mind and my heart. I knew that a commitment to missions could move my family and me around the world and shatter our comfort zone, but I also knew that God had placed a burden for the nations in my heart. Nothing would do for me but totally sold-out, radical commitment. I knew we had to follow His call to missions.

Many future missionaries were faithfully serving God as deacons, Sunday school teachers, and lay leaders in church positions when God surprised them with a call to missions. Some missionaries had been in thriving pastorates or tenured seminary careers when God called them. Certainly, God has called every Christian to salvation, holiness, discipleship, and service. This is the expected and natural progression in the Christian life. Indeed, it is an encouraging sign of development when the question "Is God calling me to missions?" begins to frequent a Christian's quiet times. Spiritual growth is evident because a sincere desire to glorify God and deny self is beginning to develop. But when considering service in another country or among people of another culture, we begin to ask questions about the missionary call.

Some Christians genuinely wrestle with the missionary call, but come to understand that God is calling them to stay and serve in their current location. For others, this call to go will not go away. They see it written between the lines as they read their Bibles. The question of the missionary call is on their mind when they watch the news or when they examine their career paths. They wonder whether they will finally get to the top and realize that they leaned the ladder against the wrong wall. They ask questions like, "Should I go into missions? Who should go? Is God calling me? What is the missionary call?" Yet, it does not have to be as mysterious as many have made it.

THE NEED

Some sincere, tenderhearted believers mistakenly assume that a burden for the need is the missionary call. God brings an awareness of the needs in the world to many Christians, but the need is not the call. If you go to the mission field basing your call on the need, you may come to see that the need was not as great as you once thought and begin to wonder why you have come, or why you have stayed. Some missionaries depart with a "calling" based on the need, arrive on the field, and find that there are numerous missionaries and agencies already seeking to meet the need. Perhaps when the need that so motivated you is met, the question of whether to *remain* will quickly replace the old question about whether to *go*.

Still, there are great needs and God often uses an awareness of the need to burden us to action. One-third of the planet's population, over two billion people, has never heard the gospel.[1] And of that number, over 50,000 die daily, separated from God forever.[2] As has been said, one definition of a missionary is someone who never gets used to the sound of pagan footsteps on their way to a Christless eternity. The sounds of those footsteps echo in their minds and haunt their waking dreams. One should not go driven by the need alone, but God often uses the need as a starting place to awaken us to His call.

THE COMMANDS OF CHRIST

Of course, an awareness of the commands of Christ motivates every sincere Christian. Jesus commanded us to go and make disciples of the ethnic groups of the world in Matthew 28:18–20. But, aren't we through with that by now? Haven't we won people to Christ, trained disciples, and established churches in all the nations in the last two thousand years? We are used to thinking of this command to preach the gospel in every *nation*, as if the geopolitical entities on our world maps were what Jesus had in mind. Jesus said to make disciples in *panta ta ethne* in the original Greek version of the Great Commission. *Panta* is a word that means "all," *ta* is the definite article "the," and *ethne* is the word we translate "nations"; the word *ethnic* is obvious in it. This word shows up repeatedly in the New Testament and since our Bibles normally translate it as *nations*, many people must assume that God looks down from heaven and sees heavy black lines around large pieces of real estate on the continents of the planet. While this is an exaggeration, of course, many missions strategies and priorities do not reflect Jesus' emphasis when He spoke in the Great Commission of ethnolinguistic groups.

Jesus gave us the command, the church as the missionary force, and the promise that He would be with us in the fulfillment of it. His Great Commission is similar to Joshua's marching orders. After the forty years of wandering in the wilderness, God revealed to Moses he was not going into the Promised Land and told him to appoint Joshua as the next leader of Israel. Joshua's commission was to lead the people across the Jordan into Canaan and conquer the land. In Joshua 13:1, the Lord spoke to Joshua, "You are old and advanced in years, and there remains yet very much land to possess." God gave him the command, Israel for an army, and His promise to be with him in the fulfilling of the commission. Israel was not then and is not today a large country. With God's command, God's people, God's presence, and God's blessings, one wonders why Joshua could not have accomplished what God told him to do in the course of his lifetime. Before we judge too harshly, we should remember that we have had our commission for 2,000 years, and much of "the land" remains to be possessed.

Some might say that this is not a fair comparison and the reason that we have not finished the Great Commission is because we live in a gospel-hostile world where there are many countries to reach. Furthermore, we are few in comparison with the religions of the world. However, it is hard to imagine why we still have not reached one-third of the people in our world with the gospel. In 1896, in Atlanta, Georgia, a man was working in his laboratory mixing together water, flavoring, and sugar. He invented a drink that he called Coca-Cola. It cost him about $70 to develop and market his product that first year and he only made about $50. To be $20 in the red in 1896 was a tough financial loss. Nonetheless, he continued to sell his product. A few years later they developed a process to bottle the drink so that people could enjoy it at home or on picnics and the popularity grew. Today, 112 years later, 94% of the people in the world recognize the Coca-Cola logo and product.[3] In 112 years, we can reach the world for profit's sake, but we cannot do it for the glory of God in 2,000 years. The keen awareness of the commands of Christ to take the gospel message to the world and our failure to do so are key components of the missionary call for many. Christ's Great Commission is for the church to be involved in reaching and teaching the nations. Every believer is to pray for the nations and support the cause of missions, but not every believer is called to leave his homeland and go overseas. Some will help send and support, and others will go and tell.

A PASSIONATE DESIRE LEADING TO ACTION

This awareness of the needs and the Christian's responsibility progresses to the next step in the lives of many. When the devastating tsunami hit the shores of several Asian countries and took about 250,000 lives in 2004, virtually everyone in the world became aware of the disaster. Compassionate concern joined that awareness in the lives of countless believers and they went on mission trips, raised funds, and organized relief efforts. Likewise, many Christians are aware of the billions who have never heard the gospel and those among them who die without Christ every day. This concern is a constant burden in their lives. Like a stone in their shoe, it is ever on their minds no matter where they go or what they do. Their hearts reverberate with the cries of those who are being born into, live in, and die in darkness. They are concerned for the young girls whose parents sell them into sexual slavery to provide for the family. They are concerned for the millions of street children and their hopeless existence. Most of all, they are concerned for the glory of God. Their concern makes them wonder how they can live a holy life in faithfulness to God's commands if they do not live in reckless abandon and radical fulfillment of the Great Commandments and the Great Commission. Of course, not for all, but for many, the concern touches that part of their hearts where radical commitment lives.

In every church, about 20 percent of the people give 80 percent of the funds, about 20 percent of the people perform 80 percent of the work and ministry, and about 20 percent of the people cause about 80 percent of the problems—hopefully, not the same 20 percent! The good 20-percenters are the faithfully committed few. Pastors know the men and women in their churches who can always be depended on to help out in times of need. Their attitude is, "Yes, of course, Pastor, I will help. Now, what is it that you need me to do?" That should always be our attitude when we approach the Lord. It should already be a settled determination to do His perfect will, whatever it may be. Our only desire should be to know clearly what it is. Thomas Hale wrote, "God's call doesn't register in a vacuum; only a person who is committed to doing God's will can receive a call."[4] The last question I ask myself each morning as I finish my quiet time is, "What is it that is not being done, that ought to be done, and if it were done, would result in greater glory to Christ and the advance of His Kingdom?"

The people whom God is calling to missions are the ones who have an awareness of the needs of the nations and an awareness of the commands of Christ. They are concerned and burdened for the needs that they see, and they are committed to do whatever the Lord tells them to do. Whether or not to follow Him is never in doubt. They long to make His name known and praised around the world. They are committed to living a holy life for God's glory. They know that it will require sacrificial living for the lost peoples of the world to become committed to Christ as King. The tsunami caused some to change their vacation plans and others to write a check. I know of a number of people on the mission field right now who changed more than their vacation plans.

I can remember some students from when I was in seminary who would not go to chapel on "missions day" for fear that God might call them to missions. They already had their life planned out and their plan did not include missions. When I worked with young people in a local church, I remember some of them telling me that they were nervous about surrendering 100 percent to God. When I asked why, they would respond with something like, "I am afraid that if I do, then God will call me to be a missionary in Africa and I don't want to be a missionary." It amazes me that some see God having to force people to live the greatest life imaginable. As seminary graduation approached, a friend in the cafeteria asked me what our plans were after graduation. I told him that we were planning to be missionaries in Ecuador and that I had come to seminary to prepare myself for this service. He began to tell me how impressed he was and how challenged he was by our selfless sacrifice. I was perplexed at first until it became clear that he just did not understand. I told him that he had it all wrong. I was so excited about getting to be a missionary that for me the greatest sacrifice and hardship would be if the mission board turned us down and told us that we could not be missionaries! When God calls His child to live the life of a missionary, He gives him the desire with the calling.

In addition, the Lord gives a spiritual gift to every true believer (1 Corinthians 12). However, in addition to the gift itself, I believe that each believer has a passion area for the exercise of his gift. A young man may have the gift of teaching and find great freedom and affirmation as he teaches young adults. Yet, when he has the opportunity to teach preschool children or senior adults, he finds this expression of his gifts taxing and tedious. In the same way, for instance, someone could thoroughly enjoy the evangelism opportunities of international contexts much more than going on cold calls during

Tuesday evening outreach at church.

Psalm 37:4 says, "Delight yourself in the LORD, and He will give you the desires of your heart." I think that this verse teaches at least two important truths. One is that the source of the desires in the heart of a person who is delighting himself in the Lord is God Himself. When we are delighting ourselves in Him, He places desires in our hearts that He wants to fulfill. When our hearts are right, He guides us by giving us godly desires. The second truth is that God gave us the desire because He wants to fulfill it. So, one can legitimately say that God guides us by our desires when we are delighting ourselves in Him. Of course, a person who is delighting himself in sin cannot claim this verse. Therefore, in discerning this missionary call, the question is often, "What do you desire to do?"

While a passionate desire and commitment to be a missionary is an indicator of God's guidance in that direction, a true call will have other markers. The believers in your home church should also see God's leading in your life. A passionate desire and commitment to serve overseas may be present for other reasons. Godly counsel and discernment is needed to know God's will.

CHURCH SUPPORT

In addition to the awareness, the commands, and a passionate desire and commitment, those who have a missionary call should also have the blessing of their local church. When you become a believer, you should unite with an evangelical church where you can enjoy the fellowship and counsel of that congregation. These fellow believers in your local church will recognize the gifts and calling in your life if God is calling you to missions. A pastor in Venezuela told me that his convention of churches had some concern about a couple of men who went out from their country as missionaries to Asia. The first one returned after a few months having decided that God had not called him to missions after all. After a few more months, the second young man did the same. The pastor told me that their new policy is to ask missionary candidates who say God has called them to China, for instance, to work with the Chinese in Caracas for a year. If they still feel that God has called them there and their local church sees the gifts and affirms the calling, then the convention will send them. Many mission agencies have learned that if someone does not have a missions heart at home, nothing magical happens when they buckle the seat belt on the airplane. They will get off the plane the same person they were when they got on it. A missionary candidate's home church should be able to see a desire to share the gospel, an interest in internationals, a willingness to learn new languages, and an unceasing burden for the lost around the world. Yet, there is still more to the missionary call. Those with the awareness of the need and Christ's commands, a concern for the lost, and a commitment to God's will should also be overwhelmed with a desire for it.

In light of everything discussed above, we should understand the missionary call as a combination of all of these aspects: an awareness of the needs and commands, a passionate concern for the lost, a commitment to God, the Spirit's gifting, and your church's affirmation, blessing, and commissioning. In addition, one must include another essential aspect of the missionary call: an indescribable yearning that motivates beyond all understanding. Defining this yearning is virtually impossible. It is tantamount to describing how you know that you are in love. How would you explain to an eight-year-old the differences between liking someone a lot, loving someone, and being "in love"? To make the definition even more elusive, the truth is that no two calls are exactly the same.

I have traveled around the world and known many missionaries, taught many missions students, spoken at many missions conferences, and counseled many people seeking God's will for their life regarding missions. I have never heard two calls to gospel ministry that are identical or two calls to missionary service that are the same. God seems to call some to a particular kind of missions service, others to a people group, others to a region, others to a country, others to a city, and others to a life purpose (such as rescuing young girls from prostitution) or some combination of these. With married couples, rarely does God call both spouses at the same time and they frequently consider the missionary call because of completely different motivations. Missionary callings, like snowflakes, are each unique and when combined with others, cover the land as the waters cover the sea. Amazingly, God uses people like us to take His saving gospel message to a lost world and is pleased to save souls through our preaching.

So what is the missionary call? How are we to understand it? The missionary call includes an awareness of the needs of a lost world, the commands of Christ, a concern for the lost, a radical commitment to God, your church's affirmation, blessing and commissioning, a passionate desire, the Spirit's gifting, and an indescribable yearning that motivates beyond all understanding. In the rest of this book, we will examine the missionary call and try to find our place in God's plan for the world.

I believe that God has called every Christian to the task of international missions. Of course, I do not think we are all to sell the farm and go. If we all did, there would be none left to send. Romans 10:13 is a verse that we love to preach and hear preached, "For everyone who calls on the name of the Lord will be saved." We say, "Amen!" Yet, Paul goes on to say something just as important in 10:14–15, "But how are they to call on him in whom they have not believed? And how are they to believe in him of whom they have never heard? And how are they to hear without someone preaching? And how are they to preach unless they are sent?" Some of us are senders and some are goers. Neither is more important than the other. Neither is possible without the other. The lost cannot be born again without the gospel, and missionaries cannot go preach unless we send them. We all have a role to play in international missions. That means we all have a missionary call of some sort. What is yours?

HOW CAN I KNOW GOD'S WILL?

BEFORE ADDRESSING the question of whether God is calling you to missions specifically, it would be wise to think about how God guides His people generally. God calls people to Himself in salvation, and that call is often accompanied by a call to specific service, or it follows close behind. After a call to specific service, God's guidance then follows. Many confuse guidance and call.

One of the most common pleas brought to ministers is for help finding God's will. A Google search for "knowing the will of God" returns 6,400,000 sites. The fact that many books, articles, and sermons claim to help you find God's will for your life is evidence that many ministers have struggled with this in their own lives and have had to counsel countless others to find their way. Young people want to know God's will about potential husbands and wives. College graduates seek God's will regarding career path choices. Many times a financial matter or a major business decision heightens the need to know God's will and causes even casual Christians to spend more time in prayer, or at least in the pastor's office, seeking the answer they desire. While some only want to know God's will so they can weigh their options, others seek it earnestly. Questions like these are common:

- Should I marry Jill or Jane?
- Should I take the job in Phoenix or the one in Atlanta?
- Should I go to this college or that one?
- Should we buy a new home or add on a room?

Is there a will of God that is specific for each person? Some imagine that life contains a universe of options available to every Christian who must then find God's specific will through some mysterious secret knowledge. We could compare this kind of thinking to a football field and God's will as a tiny dot somewhere on it. The argument then follows that the goal of each believer is to find God's dot for his or her life and get on it. Still others argue that there is no specific dot for each of us and that God allows us to choose among a multitude of options according to our own desires.

If there is a specific will, how far does it extend? Lacking a clear understanding of this issue, many will-seekers find themselves in the paralysis of analysis. I sometimes ask people, "If you were faced with making decisions regarding the questions listed above, would you pray and seek God's will?" They say that of course they would. Then I get a little more specific. "Suppose that you believed God had led you to marry Jill, take the job in Atlanta, and buy a new home. Now it is time to buy clothes for your new career. Would you pray about which suit to buy or how much to spend?" Sometimes they say yes, so I push for even more. "Now, you have married Jill, moved to your new home in Atlanta for your new job, and have purchased your new wardrobe. Will you pray each morning about which suit or sport coat to wear, or which tie to wear, or whether to put on the left sock or right sock first?"

Such extremes seem disrespectful or irreverent, but they force us to answer a serious question. If God has a specific will for our lives, how specific is it, where does it stop, and when are we allowed to stop praying to know it and use our own judgment?

In a class with some pastors, we discussed how far the will of God extends. I asked them whether they prayed about major purchases. When they acknowledged that they did, we discussed dollar amounts to determine what the bottom level would be, below which God had no preference and they could use their own judgment. The argument began to break down as they discovered that their arbitrary patterns for prayer and concern did not have a biblical basis. A wonderful answer came from a sincere pastor who had walked with God for many years. He said, "When my wife and I were first married, we discussed everything we bought. If I bought bread, we talked about how much and what kind to buy. If she bought something for the house, we discussed how much we would spend. After being married for many years, we know each other completely. I don't have to discuss with her the issues we have addressed many times in our life together. When we make a major purchase or buy something out of the ordinary, we talk about it together." This is how we should be in our walk with God. As we walk with Him, we know the mind of God. We hear the still, small voice, and we know His heart, but we still come to Him and lay before Him our major decisions and life choices asking for guidance. Certainly, whether or not to surrender to missions is just such a major decision.

Some maintain that the will of God is simply that which is already clearly revealed in His Word. If we adopt the thinking that there is no personalized dot or detailed, specific will to seek out, what are the parameters of the will of God in our lives? This perspective maintains that the football field does not have a hidden dot, but is a wide-open field in which we run freely. The believer is limited only by the parameters clearly revealed in God's Word and anything inside of them is our choice. God's will is not a tightrope that we walk with great anxiety from fear that we may misstep and fall; God's will is the wide-open field.

The believer has total freedom in Christ and is not bound by anything except the Word of God. The days of extrabiblical, authoritative, inspired revelation have been over since the closing of the biblical canon. The subjective testimony that begins, "God told me . . ." in the absence of any criterion for evaluating such a statement lacks credibility and is often abused. The truth is that God does have a dot for your life, but you cannot figure it out in advance. Attempting to do so only results in either the paralysis of analysis on one extreme or following the emotional whims and circumstances of the day on the other. You find God's will by getting as close to Jesus as you can and staying there. As you walk with God daily, staying in step with the Holy Spirit, you can hear the still, small voice saying, "This is the way; walk in it." God will fill your heart with desires to do what He wills for your life. That is the only way to know His will. Therefore, the dot does exist, but you find it by following the desires of your heart when it delights in God.

There are entire books that address knowing God's will with great wisdom and counsel that are beyond the scope of this chapter, but we do need to consider the ways God guides us on our journey to understand the missionary call. How can you know God's will?

KNOW GOD

When people ask me how they can know God's will, I tell them that the best first step is to know God. I do not mean to be facetious when I counsel in that way. Some believers are so concerned with knowing the will that they miss the Source. Elisabeth Elliot wrote, "What we really ought to have is the Guide himself. Maps, road signs, a few useful phrases are good things, but infinitely better is someone who has been there before and knows the way."[1] J. I. Packer has written an excellent book that guides the reader in this essential knowledge.[2] Knowing God is the first step in any wise journey. Proverbs 1:7 teaches us, "The fear of the

LORD is the beginning of knowledge; fools despise wisdom and instruction." Wisdom from God guides us to the answers for all the essential questions in life. James 1:5 says, "If any of you lacks wisdom, let him ask God, who gives generously to all without reproach, and it will be given him."

We grow into an intimate relationship with God through many years of walking with Him. An old Tsez proverb says, "You cannot know a man until you eat a pound of salt with him." That proverb sounds a little strange when you also consider that the ancient Chinese committed suicide by eating a pound of salt. While it is true that eating a pound of salt at one sitting would be lethal, the point of the proverb is that this must happen over a long period of time. Spending many days together and sharing many meals (each of which includes a bit of salt), conversations, and life experiences will result in a close relationship. The same principle applies to our relationship with God.

KNOW GOD'S WORD

The first step to truly knowing God is to know His Word. He has revealed Himself to us in the written Word. Without the Bible, we would have very limited knowledge of Him. Psalm 19 and Romans 1 teach us that we would know that there is a Creator, but we would be without any specific knowledge of what He is like, what pleases Him, and how we may enter into a right relationship with Him through His Son Jesus Christ, among many other precious truths. Some people will go around the world to find God's will for their lives but will not go to the next room to read their Bible. Yet, the desire to do what God has already revealed is crucial for receiving specific knowledge for your life. J. Herbert Kane points out, "It is impossible to know God's specific will unless we are willing to bring our lives into conformity with His general will."[3] In the Bible, we learn that God is omniscient, omnipotent, omnipresent, love, full of compassion, and holy, among many other attributes. We also see how He deals with His children.

As you study the Bible, you will come to understand how He dealt with His people to guide them, to correct them when they strayed, and to enable them to do what they recognized was impossible for them by their own power. The Bible teaches us how God guided His people safely out of slavery, through decades of wandering in the desert, and into the Promised Land. As you recognize the repeated biblical patterns throughout the history of His people, you begin to understand how He deals with you as He does. In your study, you will see that He compares His people to a flock of sheep who are dependent upon their Shepherd to guide, protect, provide for, and love them.

In addition to the ways that God has led His people in the past, the Bible also teaches specific promises for His people. God loves to see His children take Him at His Word, believe the promises He makes to them, and pray these truths back to Him. How precious is the promise of Psalm 32:8 to someone needing guidance: "The LORD says, 'I will guide you along the best pathway for your life. I will advise you and watch over you.'" (NLT)

The Bible teaches us that when His people needed discernment to know and do the will of God throughout history, they turned to Him in prayer and found needed answers. Psalm 25 records a prayer of David when he needed guidance. Many believers in similar situations claim this psalm and read it regularly. David prays in Psalm 25:4–5, "Make me to know your ways, O LORD; teach me your paths. Lead me in your truth and teach me." He teaches us in verses 8 and 9, "Good and upright is the LORD; therefore he instructs sinners in the way. He leads the humble in what is right, and teaches the humble his way." The crowning promise of guidance in Psalm 25 is in verse 12, "Who is the man who fears the LORD? Him will he instruct in the way that he should choose."

God teaches us in His Word that we should be wise in our choices and how we invest our lives. However, we should rest in the sure knowledge that He is sovereign over every detail. Proverbs

16:9 teaches, "The heart of man plans his way, but the LORD establishes his steps." When we need guidance, the path of wisdom is to trust Him, not our own devices. Proverbs 3:5–6 states, "Trust in the LORD with all your heart, and do not lean on your own understanding. In all your ways acknowledge him, and he will make straight your paths." The wisdom in God's Word gives great guidance and great peace in the process of seeking His will.

PRAYER

Prayer is simply talking to God. Talking is natural and comfortable interaction when you are with someone you know and love. You know their heartbeat, personality, experiences, and great love for you. Someone has said that reading the Bible is the primary way that God speaks to us today, and that when we pray we are talking back to Him. Bible reading and prayer go together in this conversation. Of course, it is also true that God speaks to us as we pray, but the illustration still stands; Bible reading and prayer should be inseparable twin pillars in the daily life of a sincere disciple of Christ.

Many definitions of and studies about prayer have been provided through the centuries. An oft-repeated principle is that prayer does not change God; prayer changes us. Prayer brings our heartbeat in tune with God's own. In prayer, we come to God in worship. During times of praise and adoration, we are keenly aware of who He is, what He has done, and what His Word teaches us. This love for God leads us to contemplate His perfection and holiness. Like Isaiah, when we see the Lord high and lifted up, we are humbled and profoundly convicted of our sinfulness. How could such a holy God allow us to come into His presence? Mindful of His complete knowledge of all things, including our failures, we agree with Him that we are sinners. We confess and renounce our sins. At this moment the truth of 1 John 1:9 is so precious to us, "If we confess our sins, he is faithful and just to forgive us our sins and to cleanse us from all unrighteousness." We overflow with praise and thankfulness. Thanksgiving resonates in the heart of His children.

When we pour out our thanks to God for His forgiveness and many blessings, He is pleased. Someone has said that when a child says thank you for the first time without being prompted, he is well on his way to social maturity. Parents are always pleased to see this development in their young children. God the Father is also pleased when we count our many blessings. The recounting of our blessings and offering thanks to God makes us mindful of the people around the world who do not have the blessings we have. We begin to pray for them and ask Him to bless them.

We pray for the sick, for the lost, for the hungry, for the nations, and for our own needs as well. We pray for our children, spouses, work, churches, and pastors. Of course, in crisis moments, many people rush into God's presence blurting out their requests without adoration, confession, or thanksgiving, and God does not push them away. However, these elements of prayer are a part of the normal prayer life of a disciple. The requests that are a natural part of praying to our God include the need to know what He would have us to do. This was Paul's experience when Christ came into his life.

> As I was on my way and drew near to Damascus, about noon a great light from heaven suddenly shone around me. And I fell to the ground and heard a voice saying to me, "Saul, Saul, why are you persecuting me?" And I answered, "Who are you, Lord?" And he said to me, "I am Jesus of Nazareth, whom you are persecuting." Now those who were with me saw the light but did not understand the voice of the one who was speaking to me. And I said, "What shall I do, Lord?" And the Lord said to me, "Rise, and go into Damascus, and there you will be told all that is appointed for you to do." (Acts 22:6–10)

SEEK COUNSEL

The Bible teaches us that there is great safety and wisdom in seeking godly counsel. Two verses in the book of Proverbs make this clear.

♦ Proverbs 11:14—"Where there is no guidance, a people falls, but in an abundance of counselors there is safety."

♦ Proverbs 24:6—"For by wise guidance you can wage your war, and in abundance of counselors there is victory."

God has placed people in our lives who have watched us grow as believers. They have been able to observe the gifts and abilities that we have shown in our Christian service. These people provide a balance and objectivity that we sometimes lack when we are on an emotional high about a new idea. Perhaps the new idea is indeed God's plan for our lives and perhaps it is not. Mission trip team members often return from a trip overwhelmed by the needs that they have witnessed, still hurting from saying good-bye to new friends that they made among the nationals and missionaries, and longing to go back and stay. This emotional roller coaster is often interpreted as an urgent call for immediate obedience. Sometimes it is; certainly, God can and does use such experiences to call people to the field. However, before you sell the farm, pack up, and buy a plane ticket, seek the counsel of a godly friend who has watched your life through the years. He may have noticed a pattern of emotionally based decisions that have waned over time and counsel you to wait awhile. He may affirm you in this exciting new direction, but he may recommend paying down debt, raising support, or getting more education before you rush back to the field. There is great wisdom in laying your situation before such a counselor, asking for insight and wisdom.

As you consider people from whom you could ask wise counsel, think about those who know you well and who have shown wisdom in the choices of their own lives. The convergence of these two attributes can provide sound guidance in times of major life decisions. Beware of the tendency most of us have to seek out counselors who will tell us what we want to hear. Ultimately, what we want to hear is the truth. Godly friends with a proven track record of discerning God's will and making wise decisions in their own lives, who have watched you grow and exercise your spiritual gifts, and who love you are God's blessing in your life. Seek out their counsel and listen carefully to what they tell you.

LIFE EXPERIENCES

Your life experiences, or what Henry Blackaby called spiritual markers, are important considerations for discerning God's will. Since God is sovereign, He has sent or allowed everything that has come into your life. He has done so for a reason and He works everything together for your good and His glory. He has allowed you these life experiences to make you the person that you are. As you look over your shoulder and consider the gifts, talents, abilities, personality, preferences, education, travels, friends, work experiences, and family that make up the composite picture of your life, you can ask yourself a question: Why has God allowed this mix of experiences? Is there a pattern that may help me see how He is preparing me for the future?

God knows what you need in order to do what He has made you to do. He knows the skills or gifts that will enable the ministry and guarantee fruit in a future you cannot yet imagine. Many pastors wondered why God called them to local church ministry after a career in business—until they were actually in the pastorate! Once in their church ministries, they saw the value of accounting, management, and people skills. When God calls missionaries from secular careers, they sometimes think that their skills will be wasted on the mission field. However, they quickly learn that God can and does use all their skills and abilities in missions.

CIRCUMSTANCES

The next step in seeking guidance should be circumstances. Many believers who are seeking God's will mistakenly believe that an open door or a closed door must be clear guidance from God. Of course, sometimes it is. Our sovereign God can certainly open and close doors, and does so daily. However, this is a fallen world and circumstances are not always what they appear to be.

God warns us in His Word when He refers to Satan as the "god of this world" (2 Corinthians 4:4) and the "prince of the power of the air" (Ephesians 2:2). Paul says that we should not be ignorant of Satan's tactics (2 Corinthians 2:11), forget that he masquerades as an "angel of light" (2 Corinthians 11:14), or forget that his activity may be marked by "signs and wonders" (2 Thessalonians 2:9). Revelation 12:9 calls him "the deceiver of the whole world." With these passages clearly teaching you about the tactics of the one who would love to sidetrack you from finding and fulfilling the best use of your life, it is obvious that circumstances may not necessarily be a road map from the Lord.

Of course, circumstances are important components of God's guidance. The "circumstances" that a man was not born a citizen of the United States or that he is a convicted felon have great ramifications for his aspirations to the office of President of the United States of America. The circumstances of our lives are often a way that God leads and guides. Sometimes, the doors that are open to us make no sense as we consider our plans, dreams, or understanding of God's will, but years later we may be able to see how God was clearly guiding us to a point of greater understanding. Keep in mind that you cannot lay two people's calls side by side for comparison; they are each unique. Kane said, "No two Christians are alike either in their conversion experience or in the matter of guidance that comes later."[4]

God has a plan in the many paths that we walk throughout our lives. The path you walk right now may not be of your choosing or desire, but there is a reason for it. It has been the experience of many young believers that they walked through an open door and entered a room for a time. After a while, they noticed another door open to them on the other side of the room. After they walked through this door and spent considerable time, they saw yet another door on the far side of the room that opened to them a world of great joy, rich blessings, and fulfilling ministry. Upon reflection, they realize that they would have never seen or had the opportunity to walk through the door into this room if they had never entered the first and second rooms. For many readers, this is more than an illustration; this is the story of their experience.

TIMING

Many Christians know God, study His Word, spend time in prayer, seek the counsel of godly friends, factor in their life experiences, consider their circumstances, and believe that they know what God is leading them to do. And, even though everything seems to point to a particular path, they have no peace in following it. A man I know had a wonderful opportunity to serve the Lord in a way that he had never dreamed would be possible. An international ministry option was in perfect agreement with all of the components we have mentioned. The doors were wide open. Everything seemed to say, "Green light, go!" Yet, there was no abiding peace or joy at the prospect of accepting this wonderful opportunity and challenge. The more he examined the situation from every angle, the more he began to realize that the timing was just not right. The move would be very difficult for his family for a variety of reasons. There were aspects of his existing ministry that would have suffered greatly if he had walked away at that time. Months and years of building certain aspects of his ministry would have been lost when he pulled up stakes to move away. The timing was just not right.

God's Word tells us that open doors do not always mean we are to walk through them. Listen to the wisest king Israel ever had.

For everything there is a season, and a time for every matter under heaven: a time to be born, and a time to die; a time to plant, and a time to pluck up what is planted; a time to kill, and a time to heal; a time to break down, and a time to build up; a time to weep, and a time to laugh; a time to mourn, and a time to dance; a time to cast away stones, and a time to gather stones together; a time to embrace, and a time to refrain from embracing; a time to seek, and a time to lose; a time to keep, and a time to cast away; a time to tear, and a time to sew; a time to keep silence, and a time to speak; a time to love, and a time to hate; a time for war, and a time for peace. What gain has the worker from his toil? I have seen the business that God has given to the children of man to be busy with. He has made everything beautiful in its time. Also, he has put eternity into man's heart, yet so that he cannot find out what God has done from the beginning to the end. (Ecclesiastes 3:1–11)

THE DESIRES OF YOUR HEART

One more crucial element—a question really—remains in the process of finding the will of God, and it sounds strange to many: "What do you *want* to do?" It strikes some as strange because they think that God's will cannot be fun—or that the more distasteful the task, the more God is pleased with us. If you have children, you will understand how wrong that perspective is. Nothing pleases a parent more than to see a child desire that which coincides perfectly with the parent's desire.

God gives us desires in the direction He wants us to go, and then He fulfills those desires by allowing them to find expression and fulfillment in our lives. Henry Blackaby illustrates this truth beautifully in *Experiencing God*. He tells of buying a new, blue Schwinn bicycle for his son as his sixth birthday drew near. He then hid the bike at home and asked his son what he wanted for his birthday. He began to plant the desire in his son's heart for just such a bicycle. We can imagine him asking his son if he would like to have a bicycle. Then what kind, then what color, and so on as the birthday approached. Blackaby recounts that by the time his son's birthday arrived, he wanted a new, blue Schwinn bicycle more than anything in the world. The reader knows that Dad had purchased the bicycle weeks before the son began to have a desire for it. When the birthday arrived, it was the best birthday he had ever had, since he got exactly what he wanted.[5] How pleased the father was to see his son take such delight in a gift he had chosen for him.

God began a similar process in your life, but it was a lot longer than a few weeks ago. Psalm 139:16 (NIV) says, "All the days ordained for me were written in your book before one of them came to be." God began to form in you a personality with preferences before your first breath. He has given you life experiences, education, skills, gifts, and talents to make you exactly who you are so that you can be, do, and say all that He desires for you. And He is giving you desires for the same. Our heavenly Father gives us our heart's desire when we delight ourselves in Him (Psalm 37:4). This biblical principle is so clear that some teachers simply stress that God guides us through our affections. In other words, what do you want to do?

However, there is a necessary warning that must accompany this teaching: be careful to guard your heart. Proverbs 4:23 teaches, "Keep your heart with all vigilance, for from it flow the springs of life." If you delight in the world, you should not seek guidance by following your affections. I do not teach people to find God's will merely by following their heart because of the truth of Jeremiah 17:9, "The heart is deceitful above all things, and desperately sick; who can understand it?" and the worst thing about being deceived is that you do not know that you are. To delight yourself in God, you must know Him, know His Word, spend time in prayer, and enjoy godly counsel. Finding God's will and the way to delight in Him are not discovered by following one or two of these components; all of these steps are important to consider.

KNOWING GOD'S WILL

The way to find God's will is to become so close to Him that your heartbeat resonates with His own. Study His Word. Spend time in prayer communing with Him. Ask godly men and women to counsel you and listen very carefully to what they say. Consider the life experiences that God has given you to make you who you are. Examine your circumstances and factor them into your decision. Unfortunately, God does not always hang traffic lights at the crossroads of your life decisions to tell you when to go, stop, or slow down. Yet, God's timing is a crucial element to consider in finding and following His will for your life. Finally, remember that God loves you. Jesus said that the Son of Man came that we might have life and have it more abundantly (John 10:10). To enjoy the abundant life He has for you, consider carefully the desires God has placed in your heart.

Is there a "dot" of God's will to find and get on? Not as most people think of it. Yes, God does indeed have a specific will for your life, but you cannot sit down with a blank sheet of paper, figure it out, and map out the rest of your life. God's will is discovered as we make decisions each day, walk through doors, discern His leading, and seek to be faithful. The Shepherd has a plan for His sheep but they cannot know it in its entirety in advance. His will is discovered as the trusting sheep follows the Shepherd. We know from the Westminster Catechism that the chief end of man is to glorify God and to enjoy Him forever. The combination of all of these steps to know God's will reminds me of the children's catechism question, "How can you glorify God?" and its answer, "By loving Him and doing what He commands." Oswald Chambers wrote in his classic devotional book, "The aim of the missionary is to do God's will, not to be useful, not to win the heathen; he is useful and he does win the heathen, but that is not his aim. His aim is to do the will of his Lord."[6] What do you want to do?

45

IS THERE A BIBLICAL BASIS FOR THE MISSIONARY CALL?

TO SAY THAT THERE is a biblical basis for missions is to understate the entire message of the Bible. Rather than arguing for a biblical basis of missions, we should view it the other way around—the work of missions is the reason for the Bible. Evangelical pulpits, seminary classrooms, and theology books increasingly acknowledge and proclaim this truth. God's Word teaches that He is a missionary God with a heartbeat for the nations. As you study His Word and know Him more, you will see the Missio Dei (mission of God) woven throughout it from beginning to end.

Despite this clear picture of His heart for the nations, God does not clearly define the missionary call anywhere in the Bible. We would so much prefer to have a list of five qualities, requirements, or steps for discerning a missionary call. Unfortunately, this is not the case.

Yet, the Bible does teach us about the missionary call. As you grow in your knowledge of God through His Word, your heartbeat begins to resonate with His own. You long to be an obedient child and faithfully carry out His commission to make disciples of the peoples of the world. You want to rescue the perishing who are dying daily and entering a Christless eternity. You feel a burden and compassion for those who are like sheep without a shepherd. Above all, you want to glorify God by proclaiming His glorious gospel to people in spiritual darkness and bring them to worship before His throne.

Although the Bible does not provide a definition of the missionary call, it gives us a window through which we may look and see God's desire for the nations and how He calls people to Himself to carry out His desires. The biblical examples of a call are not prescriptive of how every call should be. We should not view them as precedents in order to make a checklist to compare against our own experience. Rather, the biblical examples are descriptive of what happened when God called people at various times in biblical history. These recorded events serve as illustrations of the heartbeat of God, the awakening to a call to service, and the response of the servant to His call.

We normally think of the New Testament as the place to go in God's Word to learn about missions. There we find the four Gospels, the expansion of Christianity recorded in the Acts of the Apostles, letters written to churches founded on mission fields, and the blessings of the Jerusalem Council in Acts 15 to share the gospel with Gentiles. We also learn there that God will be successful in His missionary enterprise. John says in Revelation 7:9, "After this I looked, and behold, a great multitude that no one could number, from every nation, from all tribes and peoples and languages, standing before the throne and before the Lamb, clothed in white robes, with palm branches in their hands." However, a quick glance into the Old Testament shows that God has always been concerned about the peoples of His world.

THE MISSIONARY MANDATE
God was the first Preacher of Good News to fallen man.

When Adam and Eve fell into sin, rather than run to God and seek a remedy for the crisis they had created, they hid themselves. God came to them and confronted them with their sin. He also gave hope to them in what we call the *protoevangelion*, the first gospel. Genesis 3:15 states, "I will put enmity between you and the woman, and between your offspring and her offspring; he shall bruise your head, and you shall bruise his heel." Granted, this version of the Good News is still in the shadows of early revelation, but it is the promise of God that the seed of the woman would overcome the serpent and his strategies.

However, even after the fall, men and women continued in sin to such a degree that God destroyed almost all humanity and animals in a worldwide flood. The only ones to survive were Noah's family and the animals that God brought to Noah for safekeeping in the ark. Soon after the flood, sin returned to its career of drunkenness, violence, and rebellion. God had commanded men to obey His primary commission to fill the earth, subdue it, and exercise dominion over it. Instead, men rebelled by staying together and building a tower so tall that they would be safe if He ever sent another destroying flood. God came down and divided the families of the world by languages, as recorded in an account commonly called the Tower of Babel. We see this story and the table of all the nations in Genesis 10 and 11. Then, in Genesis 12, we see the missions heartbeat of God yet again.

Genesis 12 recounts God's call to a man named Abram. In verse 3, God shows us that the Old Testament is not just about God's concern for the Jews: "In you *all the families of the earth* shall be blessed" (emphasis added). This concern for all the nations and His desire that they glorify Him is found throughout the Old Testament. John Piper has written an excellent book that calls Christians everywhere to recognize that God desires the nations to worship Him in order to bring Him glory. He says, "Missions is not the ultimate goal of the church. Worship is. Missions exists because worship doesn't. . . . Missions begins and ends in worship."[1] He takes the title of his book, *Let the Nations Be Glad!* from Psalm 67:4. Listen to God's heart for His glory among the peoples of the world in this psalm.

> May God be gracious to us and bless us and make his face to shine upon us, Selah, that your way may be known on earth, your saving power among all nations. Let the peoples praise you, O God; let all the peoples praise you! Let the nations be glad and sing for joy, for you judge the peoples with equity and guide the nations upon earth, Selah. Let the peoples praise you, O God; let all the peoples praise you! The earth has yielded its increase; God, our God, shall bless us. God shall bless us; let all the ends of the earth fear him!

I remember in the worship service for my licensure to gospel ministry that my pastor chose Isaiah 49 for his sermon text. His choice of that passage has always been significant to me because of my subsequent call to missions. Isaiah 49 is a chapter that deals with the Suffering Servant, the Lord Jesus Christ. Listen to what the Father says to Him about His ministry in that passage.

> It is too light a thing that you should be my servant to raise up the tribes of Jacob and to bring back the preserved of Israel; I will make you as a light for the nations, that my salvation may reach to the end of the earth. (Isaiah 49:6)

This is the very verse that Simeon had in mind as he held the baby Jesus at the temple on the day of His presentation. Simeon said in Luke 2:29–32, "Lord, now you are letting your servant depart in peace, according to your word; for my eyes have seen your salvation that you have prepared in the presence of all peoples, a light for revelation to the Gentiles, and for glory to your people Israel." In John 12:32, Jesus says, "And I, when I am lifted up from the earth, will draw all people to myself." The context of that verse shows that Jesus is the Savior sent to people from all nations, not just the Jews.

For more Old Testament evidence that God has always shown concern for the nations of the world, one need only consider the non-Jewish people He included with His people, Israel, in the Hebrew Scriptures. For example, in the genealogy of Jesus we see Ruth the Moabite in His lineage. Although she was a Gentile, she was included with other non-Jewish people in the DNA line of our Lord Jesus. The story of Jonah by itself would be ample cause to see that God is concerned for the nations of the world, in the Old Testament as well as the New.

Since God's written Word teaches about Him and His desire for the nations to glorify Him, we would naturally expect to find some definitive guidance for understanding the call to missions in His Word—if indeed there is such a thing as a biblical missionary call. What *does* the Bible say about the missionary call? Keep in mind that we cannot take a contemporary term and impose it on the biblical narratives. Just as it is not accurate to speak of salvation as we understand it today when describing God's relationship with His people in the Old Testament, so also will a call from the Lord be understood and expressed in unique ways throughout the Bible.

THE CALL OF GOD

The Old Testament provides numerous instances of God calling. On some occasions, He called some to Himself with no immediate assignment, while on others He was clearly calling someone both to Himself *and* to specific service. For instance, He initially called Abram with no specific service attached except to go where He led, and promised to bless him greatly. On the other hand, consider Moses, whom God called to go and lead the children of Israel out of slavery in Egypt, or the prophets, judges, and kings whom He called and set apart for His service.

The New Testament records instances of God calling as well, especially to salvation and service. A call from God can be to salvation, to the ministry, to missions, or to some specific service, to holiness, to live in peace with all men, etc. Jesus called some of His disciples by saying simply, "Come; follow me." Mark 1:16–18 records His calling of Andrew and Peter: "Passing alongside the Sea of Galilee, he saw Simon and Andrew the brother of Simon casting a net into the sea, for they were fishermen. And Jesus said to them, 'Follow me, and I will make you become fishers of men.' And immediately they left their nets and followed him." Mark 2:14 tells of His calling of Matthew: "And as he passed by, he saw Levi the son of Alphaeus sitting at the tax booth, and he said to him, 'Follow me.' And he rose and followed him." On other occasions, Jesus called men but the call was not obeyed. Mark 10:21–22 tells of one such occasion in His encounter with the rich young ruler: "And Jesus, looking at him, loved him, and said to him, 'You lack one thing: go, sell all that you have and give to the poor, and you will have treasure in heaven; and come, follow me.' Disheartened by the saying, he went away sorrowful, for he had great possessions."

Even as you continue your journey to learn about the missionary call and discern its role in your life, you must prepare yourself to answer wisely when He calls. Samuel heard God calling his name and said, "Speak, for your servant hears" (1 Samuel 3:10). He chose wisely. However, when Jonah heard God calling him, he booked passage to get as far away as he could (Jonah 1:3). He learned through a painful experience that he chose poorly. How will you choose when God calls?

The Bible teaches that when God saves us, He gives us spiritual gifts for the specific work that He has prepared in advance for us to do (Ephesians 2:10). Our call to salvation is sometimes accompanied by a clear understanding of what God wants us to do, or the call to service comes closely after it. For instance, when Jesus called Peter and Andrew, He told them, "Follow me, and I will make you become fishers of men" (Mark 1:17). After his healing and salvation, the Gadarene demoniac was so thankful that he longed to join with the disciples and serve the Lord. Yet, Jesus gave him a different ministry: go home and tell your family and friends how the Lord has saved you and how much He has done for you (Mark 5:19–20).

Paul's Damascus road experience included a call to both salvation and service. The Lord revealed that Paul was His chosen instrument to take the gospel to the Gentiles (Acts 9:15), clearly revealing that he was called for a purpose. This precious awareness invigorated Paul in his missionary work: "Not that I have already obtained all this, or have already been made perfect, but I press on to take hold of that for which Christ Jesus took hold of me" (Philippians 3:12 NIV). Later in his ministry, Paul recounted his salvation experience to a crowd in Jerusalem that cried out for his blood. He told them that while he was still facedown on the road, he asked, "'What shall I do, Lord?' And the Lord said to me, 'Rise, and go into Damascus, and there you will be told all that is appointed for you to do'" (Acts 22:10). Later, in his defense before Agrippa, Paul revealed even more details of his encounter with Christ, demonstrating that Christ called him to salvation and specific service in the same wonderful experience.

> And I said, "Who are you, Lord?" And the Lord said, "I am Jesus whom you are persecuting. But rise and stand upon your feet, for I have appeared to you for this purpose, to appoint you as a servant and witness to the things in which you have seen me and to those in which I will appear to you, delivering you from your people and from the Gentiles—to whom I am sending you to open their eyes, so that they may turn from darkness to light and from the power of Satan to God, that they may receive forgiveness of sins and a place among those who are sanctified by faith in me." (Acts 26:15–18)

God often intertwines the call to salvation with a call to service.

In other cases, the call to specific service comes quite apart from a conversion experience. Noah was already a God-fearer when God called him to build the ark. The young shepherd boy David knew the Lord well and walked with Him through the valley of the shadow of death long before the prophet Samuel came to anoint him to be the next king of Israel. Paul and Barnabas were already faithful teachers in the church at Syrian Antioch when the Holy Spirit told the church to set them apart for the missionary work to which He had called them (Acts 13:1–2). Clearly, the Bible teaches that God may call some to both Himself and specific service in the same experience while others walk faithfully for years before He calls them to the next step.

THE BIBLE AND THE MISSIONARY CALL

Some who are struggling with the missionary call look to the Bible for guidance to understand the call. They see that God spoke audibly to many of those He called and conclude that a genuine call must include a personal and direct supernatural encounter with God—a voice, a burning bush, a great fish, or perhaps a vision. Not only is that a mistaken assumption for their own lives, but many times they also misunderstand what is occurring in the biblical passage. Thus, many confuse the call with guidance. These are two distinct aspects of how God leads. God's calling and gifts are irrevocable, but their expression is dynamic and ever-changing. Some read of Paul's Macedonian vision and interpret this as representative of a legitimate—and biblically prescribed—missionary call.

> And a vision appeared to Paul in the night: a man of Macedonia was standing there, urging him and saying, "Come over to Macedonia and help us." And when Paul had seen the vision, immediately we sought to go on into Macedonia, concluding that God had called us to preach the gospel to them. (Acts 16:9–10)

This is not a missionary call. Not only had Paul already been a missionary for years when he received the vision, he was on a missionary journey at the time! This vision is a clear illustration of God's guidance of those He has already called.

Jesus had commissioned Paul to take the gospel to the Gentiles. When the Holy Spirit said to set him and Barnabas apart for missions, he did not go kicking and screaming. Rather, his attitude was, "Yes, Lord! Now, what do You want me to do?" Paul accepted the direction that the Holy Spirit gave the church in Syrian Antioch and became the greatest missionary the world has ever known. While his personal call came directly from the Lord in a vision, with an audible voice and through miraculous circumstances, we must keep in mind that this experience was descriptive of what happened to Paul, not prescriptive of how every missionary call should be.

As pointed out earlier, there is no biblical definition of a missionary call; some are surprised, in addition, that no biblical passage explains the necessary components of one. Because of this, many have declared that a call is not necessary and that it is simply a vocational option in the same manner as being a banker or plumber. Others have felt the freedom to find their own definition in their interpretation of passages treating the calling of prophets and disciples. Still others say that every Christian has already received a missionary call with their call to salvation. What we can say for sure is that, at the very least, God calls every Christian to live with a missionary heart. Consider the tasks Jesus gave those of us who are His disciples: the Great Commission, the Great Commandments, and the Great Compassion.

THE GREAT COMMISSION, THE GREAT COMMANDMENTS, AND THE GREAT COMPASSION

The Great Commission is the command of Jesus to go to the nations and make disciples. Every Gospel and the book of Acts records it (Matthew 28:18–20; Mark 16:15, 16; Luke 24:47; John 20:21; Acts 1:8). Matthew's version is a favorite passage for many.

And Jesus came and said to them, "All authority in heaven and on earth has been given to me. Go therefore and make disciples of all nations, baptizing them in the name of the Father and of the Son and of the Holy Spirit, teaching them to observe all that I have commanded you. And behold, I am with you always, to the end of the age." (Matthew 28:18–20)

With these words, Jesus commanded His followers to go to the nations and proclaim the gospel message. The imperative verb in the passage is the word "make disciples," not "go," as it appears to be in English; "going" is assumed in the command. We have already observed that Jesus' emphasis is not on geopolitical nations, or countries, but people groups. The word in the original language is *ethne*, which gives us our English word "ethnic." It is clear that Jesus is commanding His people to make disciples among the people groups of the world—of which there are many thousands more than nations. Some would say that this is the only biblical call, and therefore the only one we need. Here Jesus is telling us to make disciples among all people groups by teaching them to obey everything that He has commanded us.

We find the *Great Commandments* in Matthew 22:33–40.

And when the crowd heard it, they were astonished at his teaching. But when the Pharisees heard that he had silenced the Sadducees, they gathered together. And one of them, a lawyer, asked him a question to test him. "Teacher, which is the great commandment in the Law?" And he said to him, "You shall love the Lord your God with all your heart and with all your soul and with all your mind. This is the great and first commandment. And a second is like it: You shall love your neighbor as yourself. On these two commandments depend all the Law and the Prophets."

In chapter 2, we saw the need to know God and His Word as beginning steps in the journey to know His will. The more you learn about God, the more you will love Him. Even so, loving God more than we love ourselves is not easy or automatic. Martin Luther reasoned that if to love the Lord your God with all your heart, with all your soul, and with all your mind is the greatest commandment, then not to do so must be the greatest sin.

What many find just as difficult is to love our neighbor as ourselves. Not only are the Law and Prophets summed up in keeping these two commandments, we see the beginning of the missionary call in them as well. When you love the Lord, you long to glorify Him and see the nations fall at His feet in worship. When you love your neighbor as yourself, you share the gospel with him and seek to meet his needs in every way you can, which includes seeing him fall at Jesus' feet in thanksgiving for salvation. When Matthew Henry commented on this same principle in I Corinthians 10:31–33, he said, "This is the fundamental principle of practical godliness. The great end of all practical religion must direct us where particular and express rules are wanting. Nothing must be done against the glory of God and the good of our neighbors."[2]

The Great Compassion refers to Jesus' heartbeat in Mark 6:34: "When he went ashore he saw a great crowd, and he had compassion on them, because they were like sheep without a shepherd. And he began to teach them many things." Bob Pierce, founder of World Vision and Samaritan's Purse, used to pray, "Let my heart be broken with the things that break the heart of God."[3] The Great Compassion that was in the heart of Jesus will be in us also when our heartbeats resonate with His. As we consider the spiritual and physical needs of the world, our hearts break for them and we cry, "Here am I; send me!"

All believers must understand and embrace the Great Commission, Great Commandments, and Great Compassion. They are also important components when looking for evidence of a missionary call. As you examine your heart for evidence of a missionary call, look for a burden to fulfill the Great Commission and obey the Great Commandments that is guided by a Great Compassion.

Some missions speakers are highly motivated to get missionary candidates to volunteer. Even sensitive speakers sometimes see people sign up through unintentional guilt manipulation. The hearers often feel that if they do not surrender to missions, they are sinning or wasting their lives. However, the Bible teaches that not everyone is to go to the mission field. The highest and best use of anyone's life is to do exactly what God leads them to do in the places where He leads them to do it. God does not call all Christians to go.

Paul proclaims in Romans 1:16, "For I am not ashamed of the gospel, for it is the power of God for salvation to everyone who believes." In Romans 10:13, he says, "For everyone who calls on the name of the Lord will be saved." Both of these passages are powerful declarations of the Christian missionary's message. Yet, immediately following this he asks in Romans 10:14–15a, "But how are they to call on him in whom they have not believed? And how are they to believe in him of whom they have never heard? And how are they to hear without someone preaching? And how are they to preach unless they are sent?" John MacArthur turns the questions around to highlight the importance of going and sending: "If God did not send preachers no one could hear, if no one could hear no one could believe, if no one could believe no one could call on the Lord, and if no one could call on Him no one could be saved."[4] Put more simply, John Stott observes, "The essence of Paul's argument is seen if we put his six verbs in the opposite order: Christ sends heralds; heralds preach; people hear; hearers believe; believers call; and those who call are saved."[5]

God has called every Christian to international missions, but He does not want everyone to go. God calls some to be senders. If everyone were to pack up and go, who would send, pray, and continue the ministries we leave behind? Conversely, if we all stayed to send, there would be no one to go. God calls others to be goers. Some have planned all their lives to be senders and God interrupts with a strong sense of calling, burden, and desire to go. Others have prepared and planned to go, but God closes that door and they stay and send. Their motto becomes, "Ready to go, but willing to stay." Both goers and senders are essential to the missionary enterprise.

The Bible is perfectly clear: In the gospel is power for salvation. Without it, no one can be saved. The nations must hear. Jesus has commanded us to reach and teach the lost with the gospel, so it falls to us to be senders or goers. Which are you?

HISTORICAL UNDERSTANDINGS OF THE MISSIONARY CALL

THE MISSIONARY CALL has been understood in a variety of ways through the centuries, and sometimes misunderstood. Extrabiblical definitions of the missionary call have created much confusion. Missiologist J. Herbert Kane goes so far as to say that "The term 'missionary call' should never have been coined. It is not scriptural and therefore can be harmful."[1] Yet, it has been at the forefront of the church for centuries while being understood in various ways.

We can divide the traditional and historical understandings of the missionary call into three basic views. The first is that there is no missionary call. Since we do not find the term "missionary call" in the Bible, surrendering to missions is a career option on the same level as being a plumber, banker, or teacher. The second view holds that every Christian has already received a call in the Great Commission and no personal call is necessary. Unless you can give credible evidence that God has called you to stay, your way is clear; go to the mission field. The third view emphasizes the dangers and challenges of the mission field and insists that you should stay home if God has not called you to missions. However, if He has called you personally, you had better not try to stay. As Marjorie Collins cautions, "Not every Christian is called to be a missionary overseas."[2] These three historical opinions are still held by various pastors, missionaries, and speakers today. How are you to make sense of these opposing views and know who is right? This chapter will walk us through these historical views of the missionary call and introduce us to some who have held them. It will also highlight some of the theological, historical, and emotional factors that have played a role in their development. Finally, we will discuss which view seems most helpful in understanding our own missionary call.

THERE IS NO MISSIONARY CALL

The position that there is no such thing as a missionary call does not seek to detract from missions or dissuade anyone from being a missionary in any way. In fact, it grows out of frustration of seeing people staying home because they lack some "imagined" missionary call. This position shares much in common with the view that God has already called all believers; some proponents hold to both to some degree and merely stress one over the other. Writing in 1901, George Wilson stressed, "Don't wonder whether you have a call to go. 'Have you had a distinct call from Christ to stay at home?'"[3] In other words, if you are free to choose a missionary life and do not need a call, why do you not choose it and go?

Famous missionary martyr Jim Elliot was also a missions mobilizer during his years of preparation. He constantly held the challenge of missions before his friends and classmates. His heartbeat is revealed in one of his journal entries: "Our young men are going into the professional fields because they don't 'feel called' to the mission field. We don't need a call; we need a kick in the pants."[4] Yet others who stress an alternative but similar position agree with his statement that we do not need a personal call because God has already called all of us.

EVERY CHRISTIAN HAS ALREADY RECEIVED THE MISSIONARY CALL

Many argue that Jesus' command to fulfill the Great Commission and rescue the perishing does not require a subsequent personal call. They believe that when you become a Christian, you are joining the army and accepting the marching orders already given. An illustration imagines you sitting in a boat and that the admiral has commanded all those in boats to rescue drowning people. As you float along, you are startled to see people drowning all around your boat. Proponents of this view conclude that you do not need a personal call to save them; you have already received the Admiral's orders to obey. Missions historian Stephen Neill asked, "If I could not live without Christ, can I lie down comfortably in my bed at night so long as there is one single person in the world who has not heard of him?"[5] More strongly put, Jim Elliot said, "The command is plain: you go into the whole world and announce the good news. It cannot be dispensationalized, typicalized, rationalized. It stands a clear command, possible of realization because of the Commander's following promise."[6]

Ion Keith-Falconer closed his last address to the students of Edinburgh and Glasgow saying, "While vast continents are shrouded in almost utter darkness, and hundreds of millions suffer the horrors of heathenism and of Islam, the burden of proof rests on you to show that the circumstances in which God has placed you were meant by God to keep you out of the foreign field."[7] Robert Speer wrote of his belief that there is no missionary call except for the one that all Christians have received, and that many famous missionaries did not have a call. He claimed that David Livingstone had no calling like the apostle Paul and that along with "Henry Martyn, William Carey, Ion Keith-Falconer, nine-tenths of the great missionaries of the world never had any such calls."[8] Speer continued, "The whole matter reduces itself to this simple proposition. There is a general obligation resting upon Christian men to see that the gospel of Jesus Christ is preached to the world. You and I need no special call to apply that general call to our lives. We do need a special call to exempt us from its application to our lives."[9] During the late nineteenth and early twentieth centuries especially, missions thinkers stressed the universal call that all Christians have already received. As Robert Speer echoed, "There are three elements which enter into the determination of a call to the mission field. The first is the need. . . . A second is absence of any personal disqualification; and we ourselves are not the best judges there. . . . The third element is absence of any insuperable hindrance, and of course the question whether it is insuperable or not depends upon the personal ability to get over the hindrance."[10] In summary, "The question for us to answer is not, Am I called to the foreign field? but, Can I show sufficient cause for not going?"[11]

YOU NEED A PERSONAL MISSIONARY CALL

Others argue just as passionately that missionaries must be specifically called. Thomas Hale wrote, "Missionaries, in particular, are led out of their own cultures into often uncharted waters. Simple guidance into these vocations is not enough; these people need to be set apart. They need a clear and certain call that this is the course God has laid out for them."[12] Some have written about the missionary call as a call to a place, others to a people group, others to a strategy, and others to glorify God among the nations in many ways.

The changing and diverse views of a missionary call leave many bewildered before the smorgasbord of possibilities. A further glance over our shoulders into the historical development of the missionary call reveals a wide range of opinions and arguments for understanding it, from which we can gain valuable insights.

HISTORICAL PROGRESSION

An understanding of the missionary call has developed throughout the era of modern missions. Initially, the understanding of the missionary call was simply a willingness to go coupled with a personal desire, i.e., obedience plus eagerness. The details of where, with which agency, strategies, and methodologies were left to the individual's choice and circumstances. Over several eras of modern missions history, missions thinkers incorporated these details into their view of the nature and extent of a call, which in turn influenced the understanding of the call in succeeding eras.

In the church's early centuries, an understanding of the missionary call was never clearly articulated, although missions historian Kenneth Scott Latourette says, "The profession seems to have been thought of as one to which men were summoned by the Spirit and not by man, although a group, under the direction of the Spirit, might commission them or recognize their calling."[13] When Latourette treats the period from AD 500 through AD 1500, the discipline shows obvious development. He writes, "The professional missionary seems to have been much more prominent in these ten centuries than in the first five hundred years of the expansion of the faith."[14]

Until the end of the eighteenth century, the Roman Catholic Church led the missionary enterprise. Religious orders like the Jesuits led the advance, served as the missionary arm of the Church, and the majority of missionaries were monks. With the dissolution of the Jesuit order at the end of the 1700s, Protestant missions began to find its place. David Hesselgrave states, "Hadrian Saravia (1531–1613) and Justinian von Weltz (1621–1668) were among the first to argue that the church was still obliged to carry out the Great Commission."[15] John Calvin led Protestant missions efforts in the mid-1500s by sending missionaries to Brazil. Anglican missions societies sent men like John Eliot and David Brainerd to work among the Native Americans. Other Protestant missions forerunners included Count Zinzendorf and his Moravian Brethren.

In eighteenth-century England, William Carey began to highlight the need to take the gospel to the heathen—specifically in India. Hudson Taylor in the nineteenth century led missionaries to stress the location of missions (such as the interior of China). Ralph D. Winter combined the twentieth-century missionary insights of Donald McGavran and Cam Townsend and called the church to think of missions in terms of ethnolinguistic people groups. The emphases of each of these eras informed the contemporary view of the missionary call.

In our current context, it is possible to hear definitions of the missionary call emphasizing any of these understandings of missions goals—or some combination of them. In addition, it is increasingly common to hear a missionary call testimony that says, "I don't feel that there is any geographic boundary to my call." This testimony will be problematic with those denominational agencies that insist on a definite call to a specific location—although such a requirement lacks biblical support. On a related note, when mission agencies dogmatically insist on a single, narrow definition of the missionary call, it sometimes leads to confusion. For instance, if you feel called to missions, but cannot describe your call as an agency has defined it, it makes you wonder whether you are called after all.

THE CALL TO GO: THE BIRTH OF THE MODERN MISSIONS MOVEMENT

Missions historians consider William Carey (1761–1834) to be the father of modern missions, not because he was the first Protestant missionary, but rather because of his missiology, methods, and strategies. Who was William Carey and how did his view of missions influence his era's understanding of a missionary call? Carey's burden for the heathen resulted in him moving with his family to India. He developed and put into practice a five-pronged philosophy of missions: (1) widespread preaching, (2) distribution of the Bible in the vernacular, (3) church planting, (4) profound study of non-Christian religions, and (5) ministerial training in a comprehensive program.[16] Carey was a bivocational Baptist pastor among hyper-Calvinistic Baptist pastors. When he asked them to consider taking the gospel to the lost people of lands that had not heard it, moderator Dr. John Ryland told him to sit down and that God would save the heathen in His own time without their help. Certainly, William Carey could relate to a missions-minded young person feeling called to missions whose church does not affirm his call. In great frustration, he wrote "An Enquiry into the Obligation of Christians to Use Means for the Conversion of Heathens," in which he affirmed the sovereignty of God but also stressed God's plan to use means, and that we are the means He uses.

His philosophy of missions resulted in a ministry that continues to influence the discipline of missiology. In a sense, he was a forerunner of the creative-access-platform missionaries and tentmaker missionaries we see today. When he first arrived in India, he had to dodge the British authorities since the British East India Company had determined that missionary work would only upset the delicate balance of the indigenous population, and so forbade such activity. He worked to provide for his family and mission community in a variety of occupations ranging from professor to manager of an indigo plant. He was very active in his hobbies of botany and geography, taught himself numerous languages, and left behind a legacy whose influence continues to this day. His accomplishments include over forty translations of the Bible, a dozen mission stations all over India, grammars and dictionaries in many languages, three sons who became missionaries, the translation of the Hindu classics into English, and premier horticultural research and training. It is encouraging that Indian believers recognize the value of William Carey and his ministry in the advance of Christianity.

Carey was the first man to stand against both the ruthless murders and the widespread oppression of women, virtually synonymous with Hinduism in the eighteenth and nineteenth centuries. The male in India was crushing the female through polygamy, female infanticide, child marriage, widow-burning, euthanasia and forced female illiteracy, all sanctioned by religion. The British Government timidly accepted these social evils as being an irreversible and intrinsic part of India's religious mores. Carey began to conduct systematic sociological and scriptural research. He published his reports in order to raise public opinion and protest. . . . It was Carey's persistent battle against sati for twenty-five years which finally led to Lord Bantinck's famous Edict in 1829, banning one of the most abominable of all religious practices in the world: widow-burning.[17]

Certainly, there had been missionaries prior to William Carey. He was profoundly influenced by the life and writings of John Eliot and David Brainerd, missionaries to the Native Americans in the English colonies of North America. He devoured the journals of Captain Cook and made careful notes about the inhabitants, languages, and religions of the places Cook visited. As he read about and pondered the plight of the nations that had never heard the gospel, he yearned to go.

Some people have a greater sense of the "shoulds and oughts." William Carey felt the restlessness of the "shoulds and oughts" when he considered the commands of God's Word and the world's spiritual darkness. The ministries of Ann and Adoniram Judson and countless others followed Carey and his zeal to go to the nations. This call to go based on shoulds and oughts would eventually and naturally develop into a more specific emphasis. An era that had concentrated on the coastlands of target countries soon yielded to an emphasis on reaching the interiors. J. Hudson Taylor was the primary leader in the geographic refocus and is considered the father of faith missions.[18]

THE CALL TO WHERE

William Carey's sense of urgency regarding the shoulds and oughts to take the gospel to heathen lands greatly influenced J. Hudson Taylor (1832–1905). Converted as a teenager, he soon set his heart on China. He prepared for medical service and served in China before poor health caused him to return to England. He later launched a mobilization effort to recruit young people and returned to China. He modeled a commitment to step out and serve the Lord in missions with no guarantee of support, depending on God's promise to provide. The missionaries who signed up and followed him operated along the same guidelines. Taylor gave us the statement, "God's work done in God's way, will never lack God's supplies," and for this emphasis we consider him the father of faith missions.[19]

Taylor felt a profound burden for the Chinese living in the interior. Amidst great controversy, he articulated a clear leading from the Lord to go to the dangerous and unknown inland parts of China. This sense of call led him to contend for missions efforts that would strategize to reach China's interior. The missions agencies that flowed from his direct and indirect influence bear this out: China Inland Mission, Sudan Interior Mission, Africa Inland Mission, Heart of Africa Mission, Unevangelized Fields Mission, and Regions Beyond Missionary Union. Mission agencies that define their role in geographic terms certainly listen for a geographically specific missionary call from their applicants.

Taylor influenced missions thinking with an emphasis on the importance of strategies in missions efforts, obedience over caution and safety, and highlighting the role of senders at home. However, it was his insistence on focusing on specific geographic areas that caused the evolution of the way some understand the missionary call. This influence causes some to believe even today that a missionary call should include an understanding of "to where?" sometimes even expecting zip code accuracy.

THE CALL TO WHOM

Missiologist Paul Hiebert pointed out that many years of missions efforts with no concern for understanding cultures, their worldviews, or the religions they held prior to our arrival resulted in much syncretism and often little lasting fruit. However, in what he called the anti-colonial era, a shift occurred that resulted in recognizing the value in the cultures of the world.[20] Among other benefits, this awareness led to an appreciation of contextualizing the missionary message and to a growing understanding of cultural impact on communication and translation. Such people group thinking has also found its way into how we view missions and the missionary call.

In the 1960s there was a growing consensus that the church had largely fulfilled the Great Commission since there was a church in every geopolitical nation of the world. Then, during the 1974 Lausanne Committee for World Evangelization, Ralph D. Winter declared that not only had we not yet fulfilled the Great Commission, we still had far to go before we did. He reminded the gathering that in the Great Commission, Jesus sent us to *panta ta ethne* (all the nations) and that this meant every people group. Moreover, of the thousands of people groups in the world, fully one-third of them are Unreached People Groups.[21] While this news was not initially welcomed by missions agencies, today virtually all conduct missions according to a people group strategy. This explains why agencies that target certain groups look for candidates who can articulate a missionary call to that same group.

THE CALL TO WHAT

The proliferation of such ministry-specific mission agencies sometimes adds to the perplexity of the missionary call. That is, the way that you exercise your missionary call is included in the way that you express it. Missionary Aviation Fellowship, Wycliffe Bible Translators, Far East Broadcasting Company, and Gospel Recordings will each look for people who feel called to join them in their specific ministry. These missionaries often weave desire or talents to work in a particular area into testimonies of their missionary call. Some may say that they simply *feel called* to Bible translation, for instance. This development makes it difficult for some who hear such a testimony to feel called since their understanding of their own more general call may seem inadequate. The role of missions agencies has played a large part in our contemporary understanding of the missionary call.

Because theological disputes and doctrinal controversies cause strife and division, mission agencies typically formulate and adopt guidelines to avoid these painful conflicts. When sending agencies take rigid, and sometimes arbitrary, stands on theological positions and require missionary candidates to adhere to them, the agencies are able to filter out those who hold to controversial positions and thus avoid future strife. However, when the agency requires adherence to doctrinal guidelines as well as a clear missionary call, the two often get confused. The missions agencies' doctrinal stances sometimes unintentionally translate into qualifiers for their recognition of the missionary call. For instance, some mission agencies define a missionary call as the task of sharing Christ with unreached peoples of the world. This reveals their understanding of a legitimate call to be focused on an unreached people group strategy. In such a perspective, how could someone called to teaching or follow-up discipleship view his call? The agency has unintentionally dismissed the missionary call of those not planning to target unreached people groups. Yet, bear in mind that most missions agencies are doing their very best and it is a difficult task to sort out the candidates who apply. David Hesselgrave reminds us, "Availability and suitability are both essential elements of a 'missionary call.' The monumental challenge is to identify those who are both available and suitable for service."[22]

The distinction between search and harvest theology positions, popularized in Donald McGavran's *Understanding Church Growth*, is also finding a place in understandings of the missionary call. The basic thrust of a search theology is to find the unreached pockets of the world and proclaim the gospel there. The search position is closely associated with Paul's statement that he longed to preach where Christ had not been named. Search theology mission efforts aim to find where God is not yet working and begin the work.

Harvest theology missions, on the other hand, seek to win the winnable while they are winnable—that is, bring in the harvest. Henry Blackaby emphasized in *Experiencing God* that Christians should find where God is working and join Him there. Alan Walker wrote in 1966 that "the task of the Christian is to find what God is doing, and do it with him."[23] The stress of this position is that God calls us to join Him: "The Spirit of God does not send us out into the world to witness; rather from that world he calls us to join him."[24] This position argues that the harvest is ready and urgently needs workers to bring it in, disciple new believers, train pastors, and establish the national work. Of course, God calls people for each of these emphases and neither position is exclusively correct, more important, or more biblical than the other one. However, the agency that stresses going to the unreached and preaching where no one has ever heard the gospel may question the missionary call of one who feels led to the harvest fields, and vice versa.

HISTORICAL MOVEMENTS AND KEY INDIVIDUALS

The historical understanding of the missionary call influenced movements and individuals along the way. Of course, the thinking of those involved shaped the understanding of the missionary call even as the prevalent view of the call in the church of their day influenced their thinking. A quick review of the contribution of some missions movements and key individuals who shared in this development reveals this relationship and influence.

The Student Volunteer Movement began with a missions conference held in 1886. The idea of surrendering to the missionary call grew from that conference into a phenomenon among students. In the 1886 missions conference, one hundred students volunteered to serve in cross-cultural missions and to recruit other students to do the same. Two years later, the official movement was organized, and it made a wide appeal for volunteers to go to the ends of the earth. Over the next twelve years, 100,000 students volunteered to serve in missions, 20,000 of whom went on to serve overseas.[25] The numbers of those involved and the witness of history reflect that the Student Volunteer Movement was a wide-scale mobilization and the means God used to call many to the mission field.

The Urbana Conference, named after the eventual location of the meetings, was developed in 1946 as a partnership between InterVarsity Fellowship, Christian colleges, and key missiologists. From the very beginning, those involved in orchestrating the conference prayed that it would be a means by which students would commit to missions service.[26] The conferences met every three years and served as a means by which students, missiologists, missionaries, and missions agencies could come together to reinforce God's call to service and missions. Urbana served as an effective mobilizing tool as students and missions agencies came together while the students were exploring God's call on their lives. The conferences also reinforced the role of sending agencies even though the details of where, to whom, and for what were left for later. Ultimately, the Urbana format modeled the idea that mobilization of the church for the missionary call is man's function, just as missions efforts are often man's role in God's call to salvation.

Another kind of student movement, Passion Conferences, began in 1997, seeking to create a generational movement toward spiritual awakening. Birthed out of a high view of God, the Word of God, and theology, students are encouraged to embrace radical surrender as an act of worship. The Passion movement is distinct from previous student movements as it focuses on training as an aspect of the call, even incorporating missiology and theology.

Representatives from missions agencies, Bible colleges, and seminaries are present at the event and help to facilitate a deeper understanding of how students can be involved in missions. While the Passion movement is not solely about missions, it brings students back to the basics of the world's spiritual need and the Great Commission. The return to the biblical basics coupled with the involvement of missions agencies and training institutions has resulted in thousands of students being involved in intercultural missions through the Passion movement.[27]

While countless individuals have been integral in the lives of students feeling called by the Lord to serve in missions, the Lord has uniquely used three key individuals to influence generations. Ralph D. Winter was integral in the twentieth-century understanding of missions and the needs around the world. He has served as a missionary and missions professor, and is founder of the U.S. Center for World Missions (USCWM). His research led him to champion the concept of people groups and the tremendous needs among those groups still unreached. This understanding of unreached people groups raised the awareness of the needs in the world, contributing to the mobilization efforts of the student movements as well as many agencies with ties to the USCWM. Winter's influence as a mobilizer filters through the curriculum he created, *Perspectives on the World Christian Movement.* More than 70,000 Christians have completed the fifteen-week study designed to raise missions awareness and mobilize the body of Christ.[28] Ralph Winter's missiology, commitment to sending agencies, and development of the *Perspectives* course all serve as foundational for the work the Lord has done to call students to missions.

John Piper, while not a missionary or missiologist, has been greatly used by God in his role as pastor and theologian to influence a generation to surrender to the missionary call. The significance of his voice to the missions movement is most clearly seen in his book *Let the Nations Be Glad!* Piper does not approach missions casually, but makes the case for wide participation in missions. He reinforces the need to go to unreached peoples, regardless of the cost. He makes the case, not only for going, but also for complete self-sacrificing commitment, recognizing that for some that may mean death. While the heart of Piper's missions message is found in the pages of *Let the Nations Be Glad!* he has consistently woven the thread of missions and the commitment to go throughout his entire ministry. The Lord has used the depth and breadth of his message to call a committed, theologically sound generation to missions.

Jim Elliot may be the most well-known missionary of the twentieth century. While there were four other men martyred with Elliot—Pete Fleming, Nate Saint, Roger Youderian, and Ed Mc-Cully—it is his name that is most recognizable. The stories of his life, missions work, and ultimate martyrdom have been communicated through articles, books, movies, and countless sermons. His journals, published after his death, capture the experience of a young man struggling with the issues surrounding God's call. The reader is able to see how the Lord guided and directed Elliot to a deep awareness of his call and commitment to service regardless of the cost, even of his own life. His writings reflect an understanding that God personally calls individuals to serve in missions and that when He calls, He equips and sustains. Ultimately, Jim Elliot's understanding of God's call on his life and his subsequent faithfulness to death has inspired, educated, and mobilized generations for missionary service. Without a doubt, the story of the martyrdom of these five men has mobilized thousands to the mission field. Many of the individuals who have influenced the content of this book cite that January 1956 incident as the key event in their missionary call.

In addition to the individuals described above, World War II also significantly impacted missions. Many young men and women came home with a burden for missions and then returned to the nations as soldiers of Christ with a message of peace. The factors that led to this wave of new missionaries included international exposure, seeing the physical and spiritual needs of the world, and perhaps some guilt over what they had been required to do in the line of duty. Missions handbooks show a massive increase in missionaries and missions agencies following the "war to end all wars." For some, the pain and sacrifice they had suffered and witnessed for their country taught them that they could and should do no less for Christ. Dave Howard was one of those missionaries. He writes,

> I was part of the post World War II generation of missionaries. We were conditioned by the sacrifices that our military personnel suffered for the sake of defending the world for democracy. The ringing cry which we young missionary candidates heard went something like this: 'Our men and women left home and family and went overseas for two, three or four years to defend our nation. They gave up all, even their lives, for the cause. Can we do less in the army of the Lord?' We responded enthusiastically to such a call. Sacrifice was the big word for us. My best friend in college, who later became best man in my wedding and also my brother-in-law, Jim Elliot, strongly influenced many of us with the call for sacrifice. His journals are replete with dramatic calls for commitment even unto death. I once counted at least thirty references to a short life and death in his journals. This sort of attitude made a deep impression on me.[29]

Eschatological motivations drove other missionaries. Some premillennialists believed that Christ was coming soon and that they had to bring in as many as possible, as fast as possible, by all means possible. Others believed that He could not come back *until* they had accomplished the church's task. They made Christ's last command their first priority because of their understanding of Matthew 24:14, "And this gospel of the kingdom will be proclaimed throughout the whole world as a testimony to all nations, and then the end will come." According to some, this verse teaches that Jesus cannot return until we have reached every unreached people group, and that He will return immediately upon our having done so. These eschatological motivations added a sense of urgency to the missionary calling. Missionaries who stress free will and the responsibility of man tend to emphasize this element more than others.

APPLYING HISTORY

Missionaries throughout history have defined and described the missionary call in many ways. Some remind us that the Bible mentions no such call and all could go. Others stress that the Bible mentions no call and so all *should* go. Still others have said that the road is so dangerous that you had better make sure of your personal missionary calling before you attempt to go. Some have insisted that you go where God leads, others say the call is to go where there is yet no gospel witness, while others have urged you to join the harvest, and all of them cite biblical evidence for their argument.

The Bible speaks about God's heartbeat for the nations from beginning to end. God's Word is replete with examples of His people being led to impact the nations for God's glory. Although the words *missionary* and *missions* do not occur, crossing cultural boundaries in order to share the gospel is clearly seen and taught. In fact, the Bible is clear that some are to go and others are to send. The entire church at Antioch did not join Barnabas and Paul when the Holy Spirit appointed them for their missionary journey. Additionally, the apostle Paul states clearly in Romans 10:13–15 that the nations must hear the gospel to be saved and that witnesses must be sent to preach it. The Great Commission is not a universal missionary call to every believer that they should pack up and move across the globe. The truth that there is indeed a missionary call must be understood, and while the majority of the church believes in the missionary call today, very few actually understand what they mean by the term. The confusion that results from a myriad of definitions of the missionary call results in many Christians doubting that God has spoken to them.

This brief glance through some of the pages of missions history shows that there has never been a single definition of the missionary call. Some have asserted that the Great Commission is call enough. Some define the call today in ways that echo the missions giants of the past. The missionary call heartbeat of the International Mission Board of the Southern Baptist Convention resonates all the way back to William Carey's when it affirms, "A calling is often born when a person becomes aware of the need 'out there' and of the fact that he or she is equipped to meet that need. This type of calling grows into an overwhelming oughtness to follow God's leading."[30]

The devotional writer Oswald Chambers presents a beautiful meditation on the missionary call. In the following piece, he presents both a timeless expression of what missionaries have felt about their call and the tension that every age has felt when trying to define it.

> We are apt to forget the mystical, supernatural touch of God. If you can tell where you got the call of God and all about it, I question whether you have ever had a call. The call of God does not come like that, it is much more supernatural. The realization of it in a man's life may come with a sudden thunder-clap or with a gradual dawning, but in whatever way it comes, it comes with the undercurrent of the supernatural, something that cannot be put into words; it is always accompanied with a glow. At any moment there may break the sudden consciousness of this incalculable, supernatural, surprising call that has taken hold of your life—"I have chosen you." The call of God has nothing to do with salvation and sanctification. It is not because you are sanctified that you are therefore called to preach the gospel; the call to preach the gospel is infinitely different. Paul describes it as a necessity laid upon him.[31]

The missionary call, just like the love you feel for someone, is uniquely personal and therefore a definitive description that is universally applicable is elusive. Yet, there is much we can learn from Scripture and from the experiences of past and present missionaries that shed light on the missionary call. These will continue to guide us as we turn to more specific and very practical questions.

PART 2

UNDERSTANDING YOUR MISSIONARY CALL

HOW SPECIFIC
DOES THE CALL
HAVE TO BE?

"**GOD HAS A SPECIFIC** will for your life, and your responsibility as a disciple is to find it and fulfill it."

"God's revealed will for Christians is found in the Great Commission. Unless you are providentially hindered, God's Word is plain that you are to go."

As we observed in the last chapter, well-intentioned missions speakers tend to take one of these positions or the other. Both positions leave many confused—and very often, unnecessarily riddled with guilt. They assume that they are not doing something right if they do not know God's specific, detailed, personalized instructions for their life. Yet, God is not a God of confusion, nor does He want His confessing, repenting, humble children shackled by shame and guilt over something they genuinely do not understand.

Many Christians want to know whether God has a specific will, and if so, how specific it is, and how you can know it. On the other hand, if God has the same general will for everyone and it is to go to the world with the gospel, where should you go? If to China, then how can you know which province? If you believe that God has called you to Shanghai, are you out of God's will if you one day transition through an open door to effective service in Beijing? If God calls you to India, is it up to you to decide where? Or, is God's "where" so specific that He cares whether it is Kolkata, Mumbai, or Madras? Or, to which part of any of those cities?

Even after obtaining some insight into the exact "where," should you continue to wait until you have further direction on whether to work in English, Hindi, Urdu, or one of the other hundreds of languages of India, or does it matter? Should you work primarily with Muslims, Hindus, or some other religious-background population? Is it essential to know the agency you will work with before you even begin this process? Or, does God simply allow you to use whichever agency best facilitates your ability to obey His call? Must you go as a missionary with your own denomination, or may you go with one of the hundreds of other sending agencies?

What about the particular job assignment of your missionary career? Is God's call so specific that you must know His will about the job duties of the position you accept? Suppose God calls you to teach English as a Second Language to government workers in Katmandu; would this calling allow relief work and food distribution, should there be some natural disaster? A friend of ours went to the mission field to train churches in Christian education, only to arrive in the country to find that all the senior missionaries with whom he was scheduled to work had retired, been reassigned, or returned home for medical reasons by the time he finished the appointment process and language school. Out of necessity, he began doing general missionary ministry, preaching, teaching, baptizing, training pastors, and planting churches. Rather than feeling out of God's will, he found that God had given him the greatest job in the world. After two decades of effective service, he still feels that God planned this ministry for him, knowing that his sending agency would not have appointed him to it because of his lack of qualifications and that he would not have chosen it since it was not what he felt called to do. Yet, as always, God has a plan, and leads very often through circuitous paths to fulfillment and God-honoring effectiveness.

The missionary call is fulfilled around the world today in thousands of ways, including those listed above. Finding God's will in the missionary call is sometimes difficult, but the angst of trying to discern and follow God's will does not go away once you come to a place of surrender and acceptance of the general call. For the rest of the missionary's life, there are decisions about where to live, where to focus efforts on the field, whether to move to another field of service, and whether it is time to hand the work off to the nationals and return home.

LENGTH OF SERVICE

In addition to the considerations already mentioned, missionaries today must think about the length of their service. The duration of assignments range from a one-week mission trip to service for a summer, a few years, or a lifetime. In the next chapter, we will look at how God led Bible heroes in specific situations and how He guides and redirects in unexpected ways today throughout a ministry career. Sometimes a missions career seems to be cut short when a missionary accepts an administrative post at home, returns to pastor, or resigns for some other reason. Yet, increasingly, missionaries choose shorter terms under God's leadership.

In the eighteenth and nineteenth centuries, missionaries often left home on sailing ships bound for their target countries and would never see their home again. Missionaries considered Nigeria the "White Man's Graveyard" because so many of them died on the field—often within months of arrival. The costs, time required, and hazards of international travel meant that returning for a stateside furlough was impractical, and sometimes impossible. In addition, many missionaries never even reached their target mission fields due to shipwrecks, pirates, or sailing during times of fierce naval battles. However, today's airline industry offers a multitude of flight options that are relatively inexpensive. Most missionaries could return home within 24 hours with only a few hours' notice. I have eaten breakfast in one continent, lunch in another, and gone to sleep in yet another continent on the same day numerous times. International mobility allows over 100,000 short-term missionaries to go out from churches in the United States every year. Accepting the call to missions no longer assumes that you will go for the rest of your life. Some believe that short-term missions can allow some with a missionary call to avoid career service by becoming mission-trip junkies and going on mission trips every year. Samuel Ling wrote, "Not all Christians are called to full time Christian service; however, there are those who are called to career missions, but who make short-term missions their 'Tarshish' (Jonah 1)."[1]

The value and purpose of short-term missions are regular topics of debate among missionaries. A detailed debate over the pros and cons of short-term missions is not possible within the parameters of this book, but rightly done, short-term missions (anything less than lifetime career service) can be legitimate expressions of the missionary call. Some voices in the discussion maintain that the true value of short-term missions is the education of the trip participants. Others say that short-term teams do legitimate ministry and are a great help when they receive proper orientation and are led by career missionaries who know the language and culture. To be effective, short-term teams must be educated about the dangers of engendering native dependency and throwing money at problems. Some short-termers are very effective and conscientious about the opportunities the Lord gives them, while others are a drain on the missionaries who must take care of them. Elisabeth Elliot once referred to this truth with the old saying about *summer* workers: "some are workers, some are not!"[2]

THE SOVEREIGNTY OF GOD

God is sovereign. Surely, no thinking Christian could deny that truth. But, what does that mean for you as you consider His will? He is the Creator and Sustainer of His universe and there is no detail of His universe outside of His control or left to random chance. R. C. Sproul explains that if there is a maverick molecule anywhere in the universe outside of God's control and knowledge, He is not God.[3] You see this illustrated in the old saying, "For want of a nail, the shoe was lost. For want of a shoe, the horse was lost. For want of a horse, the rider was lost. For want of a rider, the battle was lost. For want of a battle, the war was lost." Even something as seemingly insignificant as a small "O" ring caused the devastating loss of a NASA space shuttle and crew. God's sovereignty means that there is nothing left to "chance," including the details of your life. God's sovereignty means that He has a plan for each of us. Think about what He has told us.

Psalm 139:16 says, "In your book were written, every one of them, the days that were formed for me, when as yet there were none of them." Before you were even born, God had a plan for you and had written down the days of your life. You make plans and choose according to your own will, but Proverbs 16:9 tells us, "The heart of man plans his way, but the LORD establishes his steps." He has a plan and is unfolding it daily. With regard to the crucifixion of the Lord Jesus, in Acts 4:28, Peter said that Herod and Pilate had done "whatever your hand and your plan had predestined to take place." Paul says in Ephesians 1:5, "He predestined us for adoption through Jesus Christ, according to the purpose of his will," and in verse 11, "In him we have obtained an inheritance, having been predestined according to *the purpose of him who works all things according to the counsel of his will*" (emphasis added). The plans that God has for you may still be a mystery to you, but they certainly include His plan for the details of the missionary call in your life.

He has a plan for your life and provides everything that is necessary for you to know and do it. He gave you the specific spiritual gift with your salvation (Hebrews 2:4) that is necessary for you to do all He has planned for you according to His will (Ephesians 2:10). He has given you the life experiences, family, education, friends, and personality that will shape you to be and to desire all that is pleasing to Him. Of course, to desire and do what pleases God is only experienced in life as you are walking in step with His Spirit and seeking His direction daily. If you follow the world and selfish desires, you create static and interference that hinders you from hearing (or even wanting to hear) His still, small voice saying, "This is the way, walk in it" (Isaiah 30:21).

Does God have a specific will? From the macro-level of God's eternal cosmic perspective, yes He does. He has a detailed, specific will for your life and He has designed you and your whole life for it. Yet, from the micro-level of human understanding, it is not something that you can follow three basic steps to find. It will not come to you reduced to a paragraph-length life plan. It is not some unchanging, once-for-all-time capsule of information that you can place on the table to consider along with all the other options available.

As you strive to know Him and grow in your relationship with Him, He reveals through His Word, your prayer life, counsel from godly friends, life experiences, circumstances, and even your desires the direction you are to go. Think of boarding a cruise ship for an around-the-world trip. You book passage and get on board in Miami. Along your long journey, passengers get on and off who have booked shorter trips. You meet many people, go on excursions, share meals at table, and spend your time as you choose. Each day you are free to make choices according to your desires and preferences. Yet, all the while, the ship is making its way from port to port, country to country, continent to continent, sailing through the seven seas according to the captain's plan that was filed before you ever bought your ticket. You determine many of your daily choices as you prefer, but the overall direction of your travel is beyond you.

Keep the dynamic nature of God's call in mind as you find His place for you. Yes, He cares what you do with your life and, yes, He has a plan for you, but do not get bound up in the paralysis of analysis trying to find the once-for-all-time job description for your life. Just stay close to Him and seek to serve Him.

DISCERNING THE DETAILS

Many struggle with *where* they should invest their lives for missions service. Oddly enough, many think it must be to a place they do not want to go—as if not following your desire or even being miserable will be more pleasing to God. Jesus asked, "If you then, who are evil, know how to give good gifts to your children, how much more will your Father who is in heaven give good things to those who ask him!" (Matthew 7:11). We love to give gifts to our children that are both good for them and that greatly please them. Parents thrill to see their children enjoying gifts they have given them. Your heavenly Father also loves to see His children enjoying His plan for their lives. You should never feel guilty about the great excitement you feel about a "where" that becomes a part of your missionary call. God often uses these human emotions that He gave us as part of His guiding process.

Many factors influence where you feel called to serve. Perhaps you had a childhood friend from that country, traveled there on vacation, or have always been fascinated by the history, culture, and language of the people there. Even within countries, a particular region or even a city can be crucial in the discerning process. While praying about God's possible call on our lives, my wife and I went to several countries on mission trips, and even to the coast of the country where God would soon call. However, on a summer trip to a city in the mountains, God made His call clear. Suddenly, we felt that not only was this the country, but this was the city, people, and fellow missionaries with whom we would serve.

For some missionaries, the location is not as definite as the cultural people group to whom God calls them. Latin American culture is distinctive as it moves with a rhythm of life and interconnected relationships unlike anywhere in the world. Although the warmth and easy smiles of Latinos may be constants in Latin America, each of its twenty-one countries has many subcultures in addition to the unique national culture. Some feel a love for the people of Latin America and, while they are unsure exactly where God is leading, they feel certain that it will be somewhere there. Those called to East Asia, South Asia, the Pacific Rim, the Middle East, Africa, or any other region feel a similar attraction that is difficult to articulate.

Those who have been on mission trips to the people they feel called to serve are often at a loss to distinguish between God's calling and the love He has placed in their hearts for those people. The two are inextricably bound together. Perhaps it was the young children and the hopelessness of their circumstances that first tugged at their hearts or the poverty of the area that urged them to meet needs. It may have been the spiritual darkness that spurred them on to learn the language so as to preach the gospel there, or even the spiritually frigid arrogance that comes from wealth and power among a country's influential class. They cannot put their finger on exactly what it was that started the calling to those people. Explaining your heart and life commitment to serve God among one people instead of another group is tantamount to explaining why you have fallen in love with this young man instead of that one. God loves all the cultures of the world, but our human hearts can usually only handle one or two at a time. The ones He places in our hearts guide us to do His will among them.

Some students go to seminary to prepare for the mission field, and although they have no firm idea of where they should go, they believe that God is leading them to work with a particular religion's adherents. Their call begins with a burden for lost souls among Muslims, Hindus, Animists, postmoderns, or adherents of some other religious worldview. The high profile of Islam in a post-9/11 world has led many Christians to study this religion, and their view of Islam has evolved through their study—from a sort of fascination, to mutual respect, to a burden that borders on grief for Muslims and their spiritual darkness. The geographic location where they should serve is not yet clear; the skin tone, facial features, language, and name of the particular people group are still not in focus; but the religion has led the way in the beginnings of this missionary call. The dogmatic fanaticism of many of Islam's millions leads them to study apologetics and culturally appropriate skills for communicating the gospel among them to the glory of God.

Some venture into the world's jungles or high mountain regions and come face-to-face with animistic tribes and clans that fear powers, curses, shamans, and evil spirits. They leave longing to return and live among them to proclaim the gospel of the Lord Jesus Christ. They desperately want to tell them of the One who calls them to repent of their sins and be saved. They want them to know the peace that comes to God's children, knowing that the One living in them is greater than all of hell's demons in the world.

Others have seen the lands where ancestor worship is common and the bondage that comes from living to improve the lives of the dead. They yearn to tell them that they cannot save themselves with their filial rites or their grandparents who have left this world. However, to tell the truth to these people, or to any people group in the world, you must say the correct words in a culturally appropriate manner. Speaking their language is the first step in the process.

I can remember the first time I was able to communicate the gospel in Spanish. Oddly enough, it was before I learned to speak Spanish. Spanish is a very regular language without the many exceptions to the rules that plague English. In fact, once you learn a handful of rules—like how the vowels sound, how to stress the correct syllables, and a few unique consonant sounds—you can read Spanish aloud and be understood by any Spanish speaker. That was my level of Spanish when I was on a mission trip to Ecuador. Our team was in a park in Riobamba passing out tracts and sharing the gospel through missionaries who interpreted for us. Since the other team members had occupied the few missionary interpreters, I stood by passing out tracts.

An indigenous man approached me with a questioning look and I handed him a tract but he made motions to indicate that he could not read. Although he was a Quichua speaker, he could understand some spoken Spanish; as a preliterate oral communicator, he could not read a word of Quichua or Spanish. I knew nothing of Quichua, of course, and the only Spanish I knew was what you get from watching many episodes of *The Lone Ranger* and *Zorro!* However, I knew the few pronunciation rules, so I began to read a tract to him.

To my absolute amazement, he began to listen attentively and would nod in agreement from time to time. I had no idea what I was reading, but I could tell from the formatting on the page when I got to the prayer at the end. As I read it, he closed his eyes and "prayed" with me. He was wiping tears from his eyes when a missionary finally got free and came up to us. I asked him to talk with this Quichua man and ascertain what was going on with him spiritually. He learned that the man claimed to have understood the gospel from the tract, knew that he needed Jesus, and prayed to receive Him as Lord and Savior! Something happened inside of me; I fell in love with Spanish-speaking indigenous people, and being a missionary. I wanted to know this language well so that I could preach, teach, and serve God by serving those who speak it.

It was on that trip that my wife and I learned where God was leading us, and with whom we were to serve. The missionaries were dear Christian servants, they loved each other and the nationals, and we felt an instant bond and identity with them that went beyond our shared denominational ties. My aunt and uncle had also been missionaries with our Southern Baptist mission board and I always thought of them as heroes of the faith, and still do. When I graduated from a college, I received the award in biblical studies (by grace) which included a scholarship to seminary.

Unfortunately, both the college and the seminary were associated with another denomination, and to be a Southern Baptist missionary in those days, one had to graduate from one of our six seminaries. We were so committed to serving with our denomination and with the missionaries we had come to love and respect in Ecuador that we turned down the scholarship and moved so I could attend New Orleans Baptist Theological Seminary. For many missionaries, the commitment to their denomination guides them in understanding their call. The possibility of serving with another denomination's sending agency, or even a nondenominational agency, is never really considered.

For other missionaries, the specific guidance for what they will do or where they will serve in their missionary call makes particular agencies the obvious and logical choice. For instance, some feel called to Latin America and so naturally look to Latin America Mission. Others, who feel called to Bible translation, apply with Wycliffe Bible Translators. People interested in unreached tribes contact New Tribes Mission or To Every Tribe Ministries. When God calls a pilot who wants to serve the Lord with his flying skills and cockpit experience, he usually calls Missionary Aviation Fellowship or JAARS. Of course, other agencies provide opportunities in each of these areas; these are simply examples of how your skills, desired mission field location, denomination, or relationships can be part of the guidance God gives for understanding your call. Some missionaries talk about a very specific missionary calling and you may wonder whether all calls require such detail. Does God really have a specific call for your life? The life God gives you, the circumstances He orchestrates, and His hand weaving everything together create a tailor-made missionary calling. Yet, one's understanding of this calling often unfolds gradually as he or she takes steps to follow God's leading toward missionary service.

YOUR FIRST MISSION TRIP

When people share what they believe their missionary calling to be, I love to ask, "Where did you go on your first mission trip?" It is common to meet people who feel called to the place where they went on their first mission trip. Sometimes, this is due to the warmth and friendliness of their missionary "guides." Missionaries regularly serve as cultural guides to the country, interpreters, drivers, bodyguards, and flesh-and-blood illustrations of missionary life. Spending time with missionary families, listening to the missionary kids speaking two or more languages over a meal, learning about the sacrifices these families have made to be missionaries, and the overwhelming ways that God blesses them in the process are major influences in the life of the visitor.

The first time out of your country can be a frightening experience; everything that was normal to your everyday life is disappearing with the USA shoreline behind the plane as it climbs to cruising altitude. You wonder what the food will be like and whether the candy bars you stashed in your suitcase will be enough to get you through two weeks out of the country. You mentally rehearse the list of dos and don'ts that the missionary gave you: don't drink the water but do eat what they give you in homes—accompanied by the missionary prayers, "Lord, I'll put it down if you'll keep it down!" and, "Where He leads me I will follow, what He feeds me I will swallow."

However, the nervousness turns to delight as the missionaries collect you and your team, take you to a comfortable hotel, and supply you with water and rest. On your first trip out of the hotel, you are wide-eyed and marveling at the beauty of the country, the suicidal traffic rules, the devastating poverty, the hopelessness in the eyes of the beggars, and the warm friendliness of the nationals at church. Adjusting to life there requires a learning curve that goes virtually straight up.

Every day of the first week fills your journal with firsts. The first time you ate durian—and the last, by the way! The first time you communicated with someone who did not speak your language by simply pointing at your favorite verses in your Bible and finding them in his, and vice versa. The first time you sang "Victory in Jesus" by reading the words phonetically in a language you did not know so you could make a joyful noise. The first time you crossed a river in a dugout canoe to get to church in the jungle. The first time in a church service where a fight broke out between two dogs that had been sleeping under the pews. You will never forget the first time a family grandmother knelt and washed your feet to thank you for bringing the gospel message to her village—never.

At the end of your short-term trip, you head to the airport to return to your "normal" life, only it does not seem quite as normal as it did. Your heart breaks as you get on the plane and leave behind new believers, disciples who have not been discipled, and brothers, sisters, and friends. Somewhere on the trip home, you realize that your life will never be the same again. You want to come back again and serve God among these people. You want to learn their language and life, their culture and customs, and their love for food and fun. You know that God is calling you to be a missionary in this place, to these people, for His glory. Then, you realize something else: you never touched your candy bars.

God works all of this, and similar experiences, into the missionary calling for many people. They discover where God is calling them; they find the language He wants them to learn, the religious background with which they must become familiar, the missionaries with whom they will serve, and the sending agency. They begin to share their missionary call. The missionary call that once seemed so elusive is now what gets them up every day and keeps them going through whatever is necessary so they can return. As they share, people say to them, "Your missionary calling sounds pretty specific and completely thought out. How can you be so sure?" Others will say, "You're only so excited because you went there on a mission trip. That will wear off." Is that a fair and accurate assessment of an emotional state? Is it only because you went there, or did God use that trip and the resulting excitement to call you to what He wants you to do? What if you go on another mission trip to another place? Will it impress you the same way? That is rarely the case. God often seems to use the first-time mission trip experience to move people—emotionally and literally. Is the residual emotional high after a mission trip purely a human reaction or a response to His call? Remember, God is sovereign, and the mission trip, the people you met, the food you ate, and the experiences you had are ways that He shapes your desires. This sounds like a pretty complicated, detailed, and specific will. It is, and He is in control, guiding you each step of the way.

As you contemplate your experiences and newfound desires, you find that your world has narrowed to a zip code on the planet where a particular people group lives who need the gospel. This place and these people have captured your heart and fired your imagination. You will never be the same, and you are glad about it. God uses many factors to influence a burden for the nations. Sometimes it is a language, world religion, friends from or travel to certain countries, or some unnamed divine drawing process. Through any one of these or some combination, God begins to give us desires that will lead down a very specific path He has planned for us to walk.

TIMING
AND THE
MISSIONARY CALL

TIMING IS EVERYTHING. This rule applies to everything from comedy to trapeze acts. It also applies to the missionary call in two primary areas. The first concerns the need to understand the essential difference between the missionary call and God's guidance. There is no doubt that God calls His people to join Him in missions, but how is that distinct from the specific ways He leads them to do so over time? The second aspect of timing and the missionary call concerns those who are eager to get started in missions, yet find themselves delayed for one reason or another. Why could God be delaying your missions service and what should you do while waiting?

In one sense, the missionary call is a lifetime call. However, the ways in which you may fulfill that call will vary throughout your life. The burden for the nations, the desire to share the gospel with lost people, and the yearning to see God glorified throughout the world will continue all your life, no matter where you live. Paul writes in Romans 11:29, "For the gifts and the calling of God are irrevocable." Although Paul is specifically referencing salvation in this passage, this teaches that God's plan and intentions are unchangeable. His wisdom is perfect, He does not need to change His mind or have a backup "plan B." Therefore, it should not be surprising that you can find a missionary heartbeat alive and well in the lives of Christians in virtually every walk of life. I meet them in missions conferences, local churches, classrooms, and on mission fields. Sometimes, they share how God called them to missions as a young person, and they served for a summer or a couple of years before marrying and starting a family. Although they are no longer in an international setting, they still love missions and serve their local churches as missions committee chairpersons, by organizing *Perspectives* classes, leading mission trips, and staying involved in international ministry in other ways. They are not strangers to the struggle to understand the missionary call and wonder whether God is still leading them to the mission field.

The fact that the expression of God's calling on our lives changes throughout our lifetime should not be surprising. We see an illustration of this dynamic development of a call in the career of a youth pastor who later in his life becomes a senior pastor. This young man started ministry by accepting a call to be a youth pastor, and later on God led him to an expression of his call in another role. Some pastors announce to their churches that God is leading them to accept a "call" to another church. Actually, it is the same call but God is leading them to exercise their call in a new ministry setting. Just as a pastor may follow God's leading to exercise his call to ministry in a new ministry setting, it is perfectly legitimate for a missionary to sense His leadership to move to a new setting. God's timing is everything. Churches tend to understand and accept the varying expressions of a pastor's call much more easily than they do with missionaries and their international ministries. How should we view the role of God's leadership and timing in the expression of a missionary call?

CHANGES IN THE CALL OVER TIME

I remember a godly college professor whom everyone held in great reverence and awe when I was in school. Since I attended a school outside of my denomination, in addition to the normal learning curve, I had to learn their accepted norms and values. I remember feeling a little confused the day someone introduced me to this professor. They spoke in hushed tones as they said, "He and his wife served on the mission field for *five years.*" I remember waiting for the other shoe to drop. Surely, there would be one. After all, that was wonderful, but my aunt and uncle had served on the mission field for decades longer than that. In fact, almost everyone who went to the mission field through our denomination went for career-long service. When anyone came back before retirement, people whispered, pitied him or her, and speculated about what must have happened for them to return. In my understanding at that time, we should admire and respect this professor, but he had done nothing exceptionally praiseworthy in missions, and was short of the mark according to my denomination's understanding.

Yet, my own denomination's commitment to missions might be considered to be lacking by other missionaries in missions history. Throughout missions history, some missionaries went out never intending to return home. They became citizens of the new country, educated their children in national schools and universities, married their children to nationals, and never entertained the thought that they were simply on the field in three- to four-year cycles, punctuated with a year back "home" in between. Given these differing views of the duration and extent of the missionary call, what is the biblical perspective? Does God call people to missions for career service never to return or in short-term cycles? How might one's missionary call change over time?

Obeying the missionary call—becoming a missionary—is what happens when someone intentionally leaves their comfort zone and crosses boundaries to obey the Great Commission and the Great Commandments motivated by the Great Compassion.

God's call to missions includes so many elements that it defies a succinct definition that can be applied to every missionary through history. A burden for the nations, a desire to obey Christ, a yearning to share the gospel and bring God glory captures our hearts and stays with us forever. This heartbeat becomes a part of who you are. It does not revert to something else when a two-year missions stint is completed; rather, it morphs into another expression of the call. God gives the missionary call and guides in understanding the how, when, and where of expressing it over time.

Just as a young pastor does not know where he will be serving when he retires at the moment he accepts his first church, so a missionary's heart may beat in numerous cities or countries before it stops. God alone knows the ways and "wheres" of the paths you should walk. He guides one step at a time and does not reveal the entire road map when you start walking. Scott Moreau writes, "For most of us, God does not lay out the entire life plan in a single call. Rather, he leads step-by-step along the way. Many missionaries accept their assignments from God one term at a time, whether that term is a few weeks or several years."[1]

Because of this, missionaries may serve in a country for a few months, years, or their entire career and each of them can be completely in God's will. Missionaries believe that God leads them to their fields of service. However, they must keep in mind that He can, and often does, lead them to subsequent fields of service during their career. A. T. Houghton said, "If we are to remain in the will of God, then we must be under the constant guidance and control of His Holy Spirit. In that position, and willing for His will at whatever cost, we can be assured that, as we went to the mission field in response to God's call, so it requires a call of God to make us withdraw or to send us elsewhere. Otherwise, unless He intervenes, we are to stay in the place of His choice."[2]

A friend of ours is a missionary whose family moved from the mission field to accept an administrative position in her mission agency's home office. She struggled greatly with the change in role and status, since the way many viewed the change, it seemed that she was leaving missions. After struggling and praying through it, she found peace and believed it to be just as much God's will for her expression of the missionary call as her years of service on the field. She said of many who did not agree, "Many missionaries cannot sing the old hymn, 'Wherever He Leads I'll Go,' but only 'Wherever He Led I Went.'" She had come to see that some missionaries arrive on the field and, whether because of personal convictions or denominational expectations, never ask God again what He wants to do with their lives. They get there and turn off that part of their devotional life.

God calls some to go to a particular village and spend the rest of their lives there—however long or short that may be. He calls others to go on repeated short-term assignments to the same village or to many villages around the world. In the same way, He calls some pastors to serve a church for their entire career, while others may serve in many churches. Missionaries who move from mission field to mission office or from the field to the classroom or from the field to the pulpit should not feel like failures if God is leading in these steps. Sadly, many missionaries are riddled with false guilt even when they move from mission field to mission field—for example, when they move from one city in Nigeria to another in Nigeria, or from Kenya to Tanzania. But the key is God's calling and guidance. His call is for life, but the ways and places where we fulfill it and live it out will change throughout our lives as He guides.

BIBLICAL GUIDELINES

The argument that the missionary call is for life and anything short of lifetime career service on the mission field is a failure does not find warrant in the Bible. In fact, Scripture seems to illustrate the opposite. However, remember that we have seen that the Bible does not define the missionary call or treat this issue in detail. Therefore, keep in mind that the missions term-lengths in the

Bible are descriptive and not prescriptive. The point here is that there is no biblical instruction prescribing that you must fulfill your missionary calling in one place for the rest of your life in order to be obedient.

The apostle Paul was the greatest missionary that the world has ever known. The Holy Spirit called him out and set him apart. Acts 13:1–3 records the special calling of Paul:

> Now there were in the church at Antioch prophets and teachers, Barnabas, Simeon who was called Niger, Lucius of Cyrene, Manaen a member of the court of Herod the tetrarch, and Saul. While they were worshiping the Lord and fasting, the Holy Spirit said, "Set apart for me Barnabas and Saul for the work to which I have called them." Then after fasting and praying they laid their hands on them and sent them off.

Of course, Paul already knew that the Lord had called him to go to the nations; he only needed specific guidance about the when and where in fulfilling the call. Robertson McQuilken notes, "Although Paul had been 'called' and set apart for the apostolic evangelistic vocation years before, it was through a process of step-by-step guidance that God led him into actual missionary activity and along the path of evangelistic advance."[3] Paul reported his calling in Acts 22:12–21:

> And one Ananias, a devout man according to the law, well spoken of by all the Jews who lived there, came to me, and standing by me said to me, "Brother Saul, receive your sight." And at that very hour I received my sight and saw him. And he said, "The God of our fathers appointed you to know his will, to see the Righteous One and to hear a voice from his mouth; for you will be a witness for him to everyone of what you have seen and heard. And now why do you wait? Rise and be baptized and wash away your sins, calling on his name." When I

had returned to Jerusalem and was praying in the temple, I fell into a trance and saw him saying to me, "Make haste and get out of Jerusalem quickly, because they will not accept your testimony about me." And I said, "Lord, they themselves know that in one synagogue after another I imprisoned and beat those who believed in you. And when the blood of Stephen your witness was being shed, I myself was standing by and approving and watching over the garments of those who killed him." And he said to me, "Go, for I will send you far away to the Gentiles."

With such a clear calling and the affirmation from your church, the calling would not just influence but determine the course of your life.

Paul served as a short-term missionary, a pastor, and a writer. If lifetime career service on the mission field were the biblical guideline for the only legitimate missionary service, we would certainly see this on Paul's biblical résumé and in his teachings. Yet, such is not the case. Paul is actually more of a prototype for missionaries of the twenty-first century than any previous time in modern missions history.

Paul followed God's guidance throughout his ministry career. Many mistakenly consider the Macedonian Call, recorded in Acts 16:6–10, to be a biblical example of a missionary call. This account is simply one of the ways that God guided Paul in fulfilling His call on Paul's life.

> And they went through the region of Phrygia and Galatia, having been forbidden by the Holy Spirit to speak the word in Asia. And when they had come up to Mysia, they attempted to go into Bithynia, but the Spirit of Jesus did not allow them. So, passing by Mysia, they went down to Troas. And a vision appeared to Paul in the night: a man of Macedonia was standing there, urging him and saying, "Come over to Macedonia and

help us." And when Paul had seen the vision, immediately we sought to go on into Macedonia, concluding that God had called us to preach the gospel to them.

The locations where God led Paul to serve were not the only dynamic aspect of his missions career. God called Paul to concentrate on the Gentiles. Jesus told him more than once that He was sending him to the Gentiles. However, Paul's ministry among the Gentiles was interspersed with preaching to his own people, the Jews. Paul always went into the synagogues first in the cities where he traveled. After they rejected the gospel, he went to the Gentiles. Although you will sometimes hear that Paul was sent to the Gentiles and Peter to the Jews, the Bible shows each of them preaching to both groups and neither receives divine rebuke for being out of God's will. Paul went on missionary journeys and pastored churches (in Corinth and Ephesus, at least). Paul never tried to limit the expression of his missionary call to one people in one village for life. Remember that Paul followed the Holy Spirit's guidance, not his own whims. Robert Gallagher states, "Repeatedly we see the Holy Spirit's guidance in both the Gospel of Luke and the book of Acts. It was the Holy Spirit who led every major movement of mission expansion. Luke even makes it clear that the Spirit is both the Lord of the Church and the Lord of its mission."[4]

The Bible also shows God calling Abraham, Moses, David, judges, kings, prophets, and others to serve in diverse ways at various times in their lives. God is the one who calls; it falls to His children to hear Him calling, discern His will, and obey. Many times the calling is simply to prepare. Paul was prepared years before the calling came. Likewise, Moses was prepared through forty years in Pharaoh's best education and then forty years of shepherding before God called him to his life's greatest work. God prepared David with his own sheep for years before He called him to shepherd God's people. Many missionaries need preparation before they leave for field of service; those are not wasted years.

God's method of calling His children may begin with an awareness of a need or a mission trip, and continue with a burden to prepare. Those called to medical missions need to prepare for service; those called to preaching, teaching, and evangelizing need preparation for their ministries as well.

HISTORICAL PERSPECTIVES

Short-term missions opportunities are increasing in number and in kinds of ministries all across the globe. Yet, career missionaries will always be the essential field resources upon which all short-term mission efforts depend. Career missionaries are the ones who know the languages, cultures, and testimonies of local believers. They are essential for the church to be able to reach and teach the unreached areas of the world. Robert Coote explains, "In a world where hundreds of millions have yet to hear the name of Christ and additional millions have never heard the gospel presented effectively in their cultured context, there is no substitute for the career missionary."[5] Mission agencies tend to agree. In Louis Cobbs's study, he finds that a lifetime call to career missions was the view historically taken by the Foreign Mission Board of the Southern Baptist Convention: "The call to missions was viewed as a lifetime call, as stated in the manual of regulations and rules for missionaries."[6] Writing in 1901, Henry Jessup says, "The missionary work should be, if possible, a life work. If you go abroad, expect to spend your life among the people and to identify yourself with them. Let nothing turn you aside from your work."[7] Of course, this is admirable and legitimate, but the church today does not see this lifetime career option as the only biblical expression of a missionary call.

Some key missions personalities served all of their lives in missions, but not on the mission field. The life and ministry of Hudson Taylor has influenced missions history and the advance of the gospel for many years. He served the cause of missions all of his adult life, but was only on the mission field about half of the time. The lifelong expression of the missionary call for Taylor was not one of uninterrupted service in one village, but rather one of continual going. In the same vein, Oswald Chambers challenged Christians, "The one who says— 'Yes, Lord, but . . .' is the one who is fiercely ready, but never goes. This man had one or two reservations. The exacting call of Jesus Christ has no margin of good-byes, because good-bye, as it is often used, is pagan, not Christian. When once the call of God comes, begin to go and never stop going."[8] J. R. Mott was a great missions mobilizer who at first truly wanted to be a missionary. When God closed that door, he began to find other ways to serve. God used him mightily to mobilize young people to the mission fields of the world although he never got to live on the field as a career missionary himself.

However, others did serve on the field for their life's work. Julia Woodward Anderson was a missionary to the Highland Quichua indigenous people in Ecuador from the turn of the twentieth century until her retirement in 1953. She served faithfully in the frigid highlands, staying after the death of her friend and colleague soon after their arrival in Ecuador. Julia served from the time of Ecuador's new constitution in 1901, which allowed for freedom of religion, and suffered through the years of great persecution against evangelicals. In 1955, two years after her retirement, the first three Highland Quichua indigenous people were baptized.[9]

Rachel Saint was still faithfully serving in the field to which God had called her when He called her Home. She entered the Huaorani (formerly and often still referred to as Auca) territory with Elisabeth Elliot, and daughter Valerie Elliot, shortly after the martyrdom of Rachel's brother, Nate, and Elisabeth's husband, Jim. The Huaoranis killed these two men and three others in January 1956 while they were attempting to reach this unreached tribe. It surely required great faith to enter the village and live among the tribe that had recently killed her brother. Yet, she did and she remained there for decades. After she was diagnosed with cancer, Rachel had the opportunity to return to the United States for treatment. Such a move could have afforded her an easier and perhaps longer life. Yet, Rachel opted to live and die with the people who had come to know the Lord during her tenure there. She was content to go Home from that home. Lifetime service was the call and the expression she understood.

However, the pages of missions history are replete with missionary heroes who served in many ways and in different countries as an expression of their call. Hudson Taylor believed that the call should be for life, but his own life shows that he believed the expression of this call was dynamic. As previously mentioned, he was only in China for approximately half of his missions career. Amy Carmichael is another missionary whose selfless mission service challenges many young missionaries today. She served in Japan before moving to serve in India. C. T. Studd served in China and Africa. Cam Townsend, who founded Wycliffe Bible Translators, served in Guatemala, Mexico, and numerous other countries. Missionaries and missiologists worldwide respect and learn from Ralph D. Winter. His missions career began in Guatemala and then relocated to California. Dave Howard has also earned the respect and admiration of missionaries and colleagues all over the world. His missions career has led him to cities and jungles, pulpits and boardrooms, by dugout canoes and jumbo jets throughout Latin America, Asia, and the United States—as both a missionary and missions executive. Yet, he has been, and continues to be even in retirement, faithful to God's missionary call. The lives and ministries of these individuals reflect the many ways in which a call may be expressed over time. We can see from their faithfulness that understanding the difference between the missionary call and the myriad ways of fulfilling it is crucial.

GOD'S TIMING AND YOUR ROLE WHILE WAITING

Waiting for God to open the door can be excruciating. Some compare this to searching for the love of your life. When you finally find her, for reasons of military service, education, or family issues, you are forced to wait to get married. Exasperation soon takes hold. The same applies to the fulfillment of the missionary call. Why do I have to wait? There is no single, simple answer, either to the young couple in love or to the missionary candidate yearning to serve on the mission field in answer to a call. God has His reasons and His own timing. However, another question does yield some answers: What should I do while waiting for God to give me the green light to go?

Perhaps you are still raising support, obtaining required education, waiting for your spouse to feel called, or something else. So what do you do while waiting for God's perfect timing to go to the field? First, remember that life is not something that begins at graduation, or when you are appointed as a missionary, or when your plane lands in your country of destination. If you are not seeking to live the missionary life where you are, nothing magical will happen when you buckle the seat belt on the airplane.

Seek to live the missionary call with all you are right where you are. Jim Elliot challenged people to live all out for God. He said, "Wherever you are, be all there."[10] Others have challenged similarly, "It is nothing short of an insult to the administrative wisdom of the Holy Spirit to suggest that he is going to accomplish his program of world evangelism through the labors of 'moonlighters.' If world evangelism is to be completed (and it will), it must to a large extent be done through the lives of thousands of men and women who know they have been set aside by the Spirit of God for the specific purpose of proclaiming the Good News of God's love for people. They must be men and women who are committed to nothing less than full-time service."[11] This is the life we are to live while waiting, not the life we promise to live one day.

As you wait for God to open the door, there are several things that you can do. First and most importantly, get as close to Jesus as you can and stay there. Robert Murray M'Cheyne used to pray that God would make him as holy as a sinner saved by grace can be.[12] He also reminded us that a holy man is an awesome weapon in the hand of God.[13] Since that is true, A. W. Tozer's statement that "Every man is as holy as he really wants to be" should humble us.[14] How holy are you? Strive to be a prepared, awesome instrument in God's hands as you fulfill His missionary call on your life. Of course, your departure for the field may be delayed for many reasons, but if it is one of sanctification, you have no one else to blame. Charles Spurgeon said, "Whatever 'call' a man may pretend to have, if he has not been called to holiness, he certainly has not been called to the ministry."[15]

A second exercise while waiting is to explore missions opportunities right where you are. There are countless opportunities for missionary service within reach of any reader of this book. Local churches, colleges, and most missions agencies provide opportunities for mission trips. These mission trips are wonderful ways to experience international travel and learn the skills necessary for living abroad. Such opportunities also enable friendships with internationals and missionaries.

A third option is to take a *Perspectives on the World Christian Movement* or other missions course available through a local church or college. Reading missionary biographies is another excellent way to learn about the world of missions and the life that awaits you on the field. In addition to learning about missions, reading missionary biographies also serves as a great discipleship tool for personal growth.

Fourth, everyone has the opportunity to learn a language. If the language you will need on the field is an obscure tribal language that is not available, you can still learn the country's dominant language. Being conversant in the primary language of the country will be invaluable when you arrive on the field, and will probably be required by your agency. Another value of learning a language is that your brain develops a facility for sorting out verb systems, modifiers, and multiple ways of expressing your thoughts. The more languages you learn, the easier it is to learn them.

Fifth, get involved with internationals in your hometown. Globalization has made exposure to multiple people groups increasingly common without ever leaving the United States. For example, every day in Manhattan its residents speak over three hundred languages.[16] "Listen carefully on the street or the subway, and you're bound to overhear a minimum of five different languages in an hour."[17] Even Louisville, Kentucky, has well over two hundred different nationalities living in the metro area.[18] No matter where you live, you can usually find people from the people group you will eventually minister to on the field. Before you even leave home, you can begin to learn their language and culture—and possibly make invaluable contacts for introductions when you arrive in your new country. One way to meet these international residents is through international festivals. At these gatherings, you can find booths that represent various areas of the world; usually there will be a network to help you meet people from your area.

A sixth idea is teaching English as a Second Language. ESL is a great way to help people assimilate into American culture and minister to them in their time of transition. These relationships can be fertile soil for planting seeds of the gospel. A language exchange is a good way to minister to internationals while at the same time learning a new language. You teach and practice English for an hour, and then they teach and practice their language with you for an hour. In this way, both of you receive free lessons and you avoid the paternalism that sometimes accompanies such ministries. Remember that many internationals were doctors, engineers, and teachers in their home countries. They suffer here because they had to leave with little or nothing, they do not yet know English, and their professional credentials do not transfer to our systems. The language exchange allows them the dignity of giving something back while they learn our language and culture. It also allows you to learn the language and culture you will need, or at least a near neighbor language and culture.

There are many ways besides these to spend your time while you are waiting. *How* you wait is often more important than what you do while you wait. Seek to cultivate the right attitude. Augustine said, "Patience is the companion of wisdom." The Lord loves you and has a plan for your life. This includes not only your missions career on the field, but also your time of waiting and preparation. Remember that He is preparing you for service, and this necessary preparation takes time. Robert Speer observed, "A man not spiritually fitted ought not to go, but neither is fit to stay. His immediate duty is to clean up and empower his life."[19] Learn to trust His heart when you cannot trace His hand. He knows exactly what is necessary to conform you to the image of Christ, and at the end of the day, even if what is happening is not your preference, being conformed to Christ is what you want.

While you wait, there are short-term trips available that will allow you to see the places God may be calling. You can meet the missionaries with whom you would serve and interact with nationals in the cultural context that could be your future home—all of which can help focus your understanding of God's leading. Sometimes the waiting is simply to know where and you wonder why God will not make it plain. Take comfort in knowing that many have waited for God to make that clear. Jim Elliot wrote, "To me, Ecuador is simply an avenue of obedience to the simple word of Christ. There is room for me there, and I am free to go. This of course is true of a great many other places, but having said there is need, and sensed my freedom, through several years of waiting in prayer for leading on this very point of 'where?' I now feel peace in saying, 'I go, sir, by grace.' "[20]

CONCLUSION

THE MISSIONARY CALL is a lifelong love and burden that will find expression in many ways. When God provides fresh guidance for when and where, it is often confused for a new calling. However, guidance is merely the way that God chooses to use you for His glory. Since God is sovereign, He chooses whom He will use, but He also chooses the when, where, and how. It is as important to be submissive and meek in accepting a redirection as it is to pack and go in the beginning of your call.

While waiting on the green light to be able to go to the mission field and begin your service, there is much to do. First and foremost, get as close to Jesus as you possibly can, and stay there. Learn to hear His voice, know and trust His Word, and rely on Him. When you finally do arrive on the mission field, you will regularly use the faith "muscles" that you developed in the exercise of Christian living while waiting. As you think through your own life and look over your shoulder through missions and biblical history, be at peace when you remember His faithfulness to His promises. If you are still unsure about the missionary calling on your life, remember that He wants you to know and understand your call more than you do, but in His time. And, His timing is not ours.

WHAT SHOULD I DO IF MY SPOUSE DOES NOT FEEL CALLED?

THE MISSIONARY CALL comes to everyone in a unique way. No two people are called to missions in the exact same way or moment in time. This often results in a husband or wife whose spouse does not share that call. Due to family background, home church missions program, and personal experience, some Christians seem to be more open to the possibility of missions and therefore hear and receive the call more readily. The resulting tension and tears of a sense of unequal callings can devastate the harmony in a home. Unfortunately, having a spouse who does not share the same calling is one of the more common concerns that students come to discuss with me. Both men and women have experienced this frustration in the fulfillment of their missionary call.

Following the call to missions is not like accepting any other kind of job. A wife may not share her husband's zeal for law, sports, or building houses, but they live together happily in perfect harmony. The husband called to work in church ministry may not share his wife's burden to be a schoolteacher, accountant, or real estate agent, but the American dream remains intact. Accepting a missionary call is much different. When a spouse feels called to missions and accepts the call, he or she cannot enjoy breakfast at home, wave good-bye to the wife or husband and kids, commute to work, and be home by 5:30 after a long day at the office. Everything changes and the spouse who is not so sure of a missionary call will feel very threatened at the prospect of all these changes.

In my own case, I felt called to missions very soon after the day of my conversion at twenty-four years of age. Although I grew up in a Christian home, and had gone through the motions to join the church when I was young, I was not born again until I was a young adult. My aunt and uncle were career missionaries to the Pacific Rim, so my home and church were familiar with and highly valued missions and missionaries.

After almost five years of marriage, the Lord wonderfully saved us. I was overwhelmed with love and thanksgiving to my Lord. I felt that because I had wasted so much of my life, the rest of it should really count by doing something bold for the Lord. Almost immediately, my thoughts turned to missions. While this was an exciting prospect to me, my wife felt uncertain about this threat to the security of our home, our newborn son, and all we had ever planned. The tension we felt is the same stress and tension in thousands of young marriages right now. It is on the minds and in the homes of many believers today. Why are some Christians more open to missions than others? Why does one spouse thrill at the thought of missions while the other might recoil at the mere mention of the word?

DIFFERENT UNDERSTANDINGS OF THE CALL

Sometimes, we find the answer in the church backgrounds of the couple. Many churches provide dynamic missions programs for their young people. Missionaries who are home on furlough often speak for these groups of young people, relating exciting tales of living and working overseas. In such churches, young people regularly hear a challenge to consider the call to missions and go on mission trips. Many missions candidates have shared with me that they first felt God calling them to missions as a young boy or girl in their home church.

Sometimes young Christians forget this missionary call during high school or college. Romances blossom and bloom during this season of life and many once-mission-field-bound young people make life decisions with no thought to previous callings, vows, or commitments to the Lord. When God brings these former vows and commitments to their minds and the missionary call begins to stir in their hearts, some would-have-been missionaries find themselves married to sincere believers who simply do not feel any calling or leaning toward missions. In a world where some mission agencies require both spouses to share the calling, would-be candidates cry out in frustration and despair, "It's not fair!" The overused phrase, "When God calls a person, He calls the entire family," prompts the frustrated candidate to declare that the "uncalled" spouse must be out of the will of God, not submissive, or disobedient. Such a conclusion is seldom fair. The spouse who does not feel called often feels guilty without any prompting. After all, if your spouse feels so sure about their missionary call, perhaps you are keeping your family from fulfilling God's will by your reluctance to go. Of course, it could be that neither spouse has genuinely received a call or that the timing is not right, but the angst of a divided home is heartbreaking.

In the absence of any clear description of the missionary call, we leave Christians to their own understanding and the countless ways in which believers seek to know the will of God as they seek to discern whether God is so calling them. It is quite possible that both husband and wife have been called to equal degrees, but one spouse has an unspoken understanding of a missionary call that includes a night vision or lightning bolt, and knowing that he has not experienced anything so spectacular, concludes that the call has not come to him.

MISSIONS AGENCIES AND THE SPOUSE'S CALL

We have seen in the biblical accounts that there are no specific commandments or clear guidelines to guide definitively in understanding and applying the missionary call. Therefore, in actual practice, most mission agencies base their missionary call requirements on broader biblical principles and practical considerations rather than specific biblical passages. In such matters, they often appeal to verses that are more *descriptive* of the way Paul's missionary ministry was, for example, rather than *prescriptive* of how everyone's should always be. It seems that Peter and the other married disciples must have left wives behind for a time to travel with Jesus because in Luke 18:28, Peter said that they had left all and followed Him. Later, however, Paul writes that Peter and others took their wives with them on their preaching journeys (1 Corinthians 9:5). Of course, we do not have any indication that these wives had to articulate a missionary call to travel with their husbands.

In the case of contemporary pastoral ministry in the local church, an ordination council or pastor search committee requires the pastoral candidate both to have and to articulate a call to ministry. While the committee generally requires that his wife fully support the call, no one expects her to articulate a call to ministry. In fact, in many cases, the council or committee does not even interview her. Since there are obviously many more pastors than missionaries, one would expect greater biblical attention given to the role of a pastor's wife. And, indeed, we do find such attention given to ministry leaders' wives in passages such as 1 Timothy 3. However, what is absent in these passages is a requirement for the spouse to share the same calling to the gospel ministry as her husband.

Therefore, biblically speaking, from which passage do we justify requiring the wife to articulate a calling—especially when we only do so in the case of serving outside the country and not when ministering at home? In fact, there is actually no passage to indicate either husband or wife must share a call to missions in order to validate the call. Even so, many mission agencies say that both spouses should share the missionary call as a requirement for service—even though the Bible gives no clear guidance to do so. As mentioned, these agencies do not require both to articulate a call for exegetical reasons, but for practical reasons, which are also important to consider.

Rather than look to the specific verses to defend or defeat the requirement for both spouses to share a missionary call, we should look to practical missionary life and general biblical principles of shared calls. Wise stewardship of life and resources includes learning the lessons of saints who have gone before us. When we stand on the shoulders of the godly missionaries who have served and learned life lessons at great cost, we are able to see a little further down the road than they did and build on their gains.

HISTORICAL AND BIBLICAL ILLUSTRATIONS OF THE SPOUSE'S CALL

William Carey is a name that often comes to mind when considering the spouse's missionary call. In chapter 4, we noted some of Carey's accomplishments on the mission field. As we consider whether the missionary call is required of both spouses, we must return to his family's story. When Carey felt called to go to India, he implored his wife to go with him. Being pregnant with their fourth child at the time, she was not open to the idea, and Carey finally resolved to go to India alone. Although he had hoped she would accompany him, facing the imminent departure of the vessel headed for India, he said good-bye and left. When an unexpected turn of events delayed the ship's departure, he returned with a traveling companion to ask her one last time to come with him. She reluctantly relented and agreed to go. Hers was anything but a clear articulation of a missionary call!

Once they arrived in India, they were illegal aliens in a sense and working as missionaries without permission. The British East India Company had determined that the nationals should not be upset by missionary efforts. In the following months and years, the Carey family suffered great hardship and loss—even burying their young son. Dorothy Carey began to lose her mind. Some historical discussions are more revealing than others, but by all accounts, she appears to have suffered an irreversible nervous breakdown. She would sometimes become greatly agitated, manifest violent tendencies, scream incoherently, and for a time was "confined" by being tied to her bed. Carey loved his wife deeply and some have argued that this treatment was much better than she would have received in the mental institutions of late eighteenth-century England. Still, how could God use a family so divided? Surely, we reason, God could not bless Carey's ministry. Yet, William Carey advanced from his humble cobbler beginnings to eventually being considered the father of modern missions.

No one champions the William and Dorothy Carey experience as the model for missionary couples today and no mission agency would allow one of its missionaries to suffer so much without intervention. Some agencies point to the fact that in his day there was no requirement for shared missionary callings and that this is the kind of horror that can result. Some frustrated candidates mention the ministry successes Carey experienced as an illustration of ministry fruit in spite of the absence of shared callings. However, most critics of the requirement for a shared call would rather support their argument by noting the absence of biblical guidelines for it. While the Bible does not speak directly to a shared missionary calling, it does give the counsel we need for living in harmony in our families.

There are many biblical principles that we can apply to the matter of a shared call in marriage.

◆ Amos 3:3 asks, "Do two walk together, unless they have agreed to meet?"

◆ Ecclesiastes 4:9–12 states, "Two are better than one, because they have a good reward for their toil. For if they fall, one will lift up his fellow. But woe to him who is alone when he falls and has not another to lift him up! Again, if two lie together, they keep warm, but how can one keep warm alone? And though a man might prevail against one who is alone, two will withstand him—a threefold cord is not quickly broken."

♦ 2 Corinthians 6:14 exhorts, "Do not be unequally yoked with unbelievers. For what partnership has righteousness with lawlessness? Or what fellowship has light with darkness?"

The biblical principles in these verses, and many others, teach the value of unity in agreement. None of them speaks directly to the issue of both spouses articulating a missionary call, but they do speak to the value of agreement for peace and harmony. Unity, peace, and harmony in a marriage reflect in our faces, words, and homes. This common life purpose is a powerful testimony of the grace, peace, and power of Christ and preaches a sermon to our target people group in a way that our words never could. A couple zealously serving in their common call is a much more positive Christian testimony than the stressed-out couple, divided and miserable from contrary callings.

APPLYING BIBLICAL PRINCIPLES TO THE SPOUSE'S CALL

Of course, we could and should apply these biblical principles to all areas of life and any occupation. Why then do some take them to the extreme of requiring the articulation of a call from both spouses only in the case of missionaries and not for pastors, music ministers, or youth directors? Unfortunately, it is often expected and assumed that ministers and their wives share the call to ministry, but this is not always true. In any ministry endeavor, the family that feels a common purpose and calling will, naturally, be the most effective. Yet Scripture does not seem to require that both spouses share the same call to ministry. Practical experience, however, points to its benefits.

Although virtually all mission agencies request that both spouses share a missionary call, only one or two agencies absolutely insist upon it. Indeed, one of the largest mission agencies in the world will actually send couples home from missionary orientation if they discover that one spouse or the other cannot honestly attest to a profound missionary call. Other agencies are less rigid and flexible enough to consider couples on a case-by-case basis. This is generally due to their smaller size and number of missionaries, which enables them to dedicate the time necessary to examine possible exceptions and extenuating circumstances.

Many agencies will also accept a less defined statement of a missionary call from one spouse or the other. In this case, both spouses must still have a sincere calling from the Lord, just not necessarily the same one. For example, the husband may say that God has called him to plant churches and train leaders among the Quechuas in Bolivia. He may have numerous convincing arguments for this profound belief. However, when the agency interviews his wife, she may simply and sincerely respond, "I believe that God has called me to be a godly, submissive wife and mother and to provide a nurturing home for my family. I can do that anywhere in the world. My husband is the spiritual head of our home and he believes God has called us to Bolivia. I can go with joy in my heart and complete willingness to be a missionary wife in Bolivia where I will serve the Lord by loving my husband, children, and the people He calls us to serve." Some agencies would embrace this couple and see their missionary calling as sufficient. Others might recognize it as biblical love and submission, but it would be a less definitive statement of missionary calling than they would prefer or accept. In fact, some would deny them appointment with their agency.

As previously mentioned, for some of the agencies, the issue of the spouse's call is not at all a biblical consideration of passages, chapters, and verses. Rather, for practical reasons and lessons learned the hard way over decades of missionary experience, they request both spouses to share a missionary call. A survey of some prominent mission agencies revealed that only one absolutely requires that both spouses articulate a call to missions without exception. The remaining agencies preferred that both spouses share a missionary call but added that they evaluate couples on a case-by-case basis. While there is no biblical mandate for requiring that both spouses share the missionary call, there are sound reasons why this is desirable.

Latin America Mission has explained some basic reasons why it prefers both spouses to share the missionary call.[1] These reasons are not unique to missionary life, but virtually every missionary home experiences them, and usually to a degree that is not known elsewhere. The basic areas addressed are financial sacrifice; raising support; cross-cultural living; constant transitions; the missionary lifestyle that is always on call and requires meeting ever-changing needs; and the ethics involved with raising support for a missionary salary, donor relations, and communicating with constituents.

It is difficult to live in a fish bowl under constant examination while living on a tight budget that is advertised to anyone who wants to know how much you make and how you spend it. Many pastors and their families know this experience. However, add to these issues a sacrificial lifestyle in a majority world culture, and ministry where most of the people are of a religion that does not want you there, and you have the makings of a marital-tension time bomb. The unique characteristics of the missionary life bring stressors that marriages will not experience in most other career paths.

I once taught in a pastoral training conference in South America where a national church leader and I took turns leading hour-long sessions. I had finished my first session of the day and was sitting in a back pew preparing my notes while my Latin American brother was teaching his session. I was half listening as I concentrated on my next teaching outline. However, I gave him my full attention when I heard him mention the name of some missionaries I knew in an illustration. He asked the brothers in the class whether they remembered a missionary who had since retired. They all smiled and a warm glow seemed to arise from them. My friend recounted how much they all loved him and what all he had done for them. From around the room, short testimonies went up about what a great missionary he was. Then my friend asked if they remembered his wife. They all seemed embarrassed and looked at the floor. He said, "She never let us in her home or had a conversation with us, did she?" "No," they all murmured. He spoke for them when he said, "She did not really like us, did she?" They all shook their heads. Then he made his point, "She never told us that with her words, but we could tell in her attitude toward us." He was illustrating that we must be careful with our lifestyle because it speaks more loudly than what we say or do not say. Similarly, our family knew a pastor who accepted a church against the desires of his wife. She had not wanted to leave the last church where her friends were. In the new church, she came for worship on Sunday mornings, but not for Sunday school or to the evening service. She never came on Wednesdays or for any activities. She did not want to be there and it was obvious that she was doing the bare minimum. How effective do you think his ministry was? When couples do not share a common call to service, the ministry suffers.

Some agencies require that both spouses share the call for the purpose of missionary retention. When a couple goes to the mission field without a common missionary calling, one spouse often goes out of guilt, a desire to go along to get along, or because "I don't want to be the one who keeps our family from following God's will." When the emotional honeymoon of the tourist stage wears off and culture shock begins to take over, even the deepest sense of call begins to be questioned and reexamined. The missionary without the call is already mentally packing their bags.

When the "called" spouse begins to express the inevitable doubt, frustration, depression, and introspection, the spouse who does not share the missionary call will not be pulling up, but rather pulling down. Jesus wisely sent the disciples out in pairs, not only for accountability and team synergism, but also for encouragement.

CONCLUSION

IN CHAPTER 6, we addressed what you can do while waiting for the calling to become clear and defined. However, there are matters that are particular to couples. Remember that God gave you your spouse as a precious gift.

Husbands should love their wives as Christ loved the church and gave Himself up for her. Paul says that we are to care for our wives and love them as we do our own bodies. Peter reminds us that we hinder our prayers if we act in sinful ways toward them. Trying to guilt or manipulate your wife into accepting a missionary call is a recipe for disaster. Love her and be patient. Pray and seek to be the husband whom God will use to provide the security that your family needs.

Wives should respect and be subject to their husbands. If God has called you, only He can call your husband. Peter reminds you to live in such a way that you may win your husband over (1 Peter 3:1–2). Of course, Peter is speaking of the salvation of unbelieving husbands, but if that is true of salvation, it may also be true of guidance into missions.

While you wait, grow your marriage to be as healthy as it can be. Work on communication and ministering to one another. Learn a language together, read missionary biographies together, entertain furloughing missionaries in your home—as guests in a spare room or for a meal—and email missionaries on the field to be better able to pray for them. Go on short-term mission trips together. Be open and let God lead. In this way, when God clearly leads and guides you both into the same missionary calling, you will have a healthy marriage, practice learning new things together, and knowledge of missionary life. A healthy marriage and well-developed learning skills are essential for a couple living the missionary life with a world-changing testimony.

PART 3

FULFILLING THE MISSIONARY CALL

GETTING
TO THE
FIELD

THE PATH FROM SURRENDERING to the call to fi-
nally sharing the gospel in a new culture is much like climbing up a
mountain; the way is difficult but with each hard-won step you can
see the landscape more clearly and the experience is breathtaking.
The missionary call is very often defined and confirmed in the life
of missionaries as they walk through the steps to be appointed and
actually arrive on the mission field. You explore the mission agency
options open to you for going to the field, learn about missionary
life, and research different cultures. Along the way, you leave a
career, give away belongings, sell your car and home, and say good-
bye to precious friends and family. This pathway usually leads to
the pulpits of many churches since missions candidates must share
their vision and raise support or enlist the prayers of churches at
home. The process of missions agency appointment and speaking
in churches gives you many opportunities to articulate your call.
As a result, that call becomes increasingly certain in your heart.

You will also think about the step you are taking every time you say good-bye to someone, speak to potential home-buyers, or give away possessions you once cherished. At this point, the fog of the missionary call often yields to a settled peace about the work God is doing in your life. The clarity that comes in this process is the "so what" of this chapter because the needed missionary call definition and confirmation come as you step out in faith and walk through the remaining steps to your new home. By now, some of you may confidently believe that God is calling you to international missions and are wondering about the next steps. Let me encourage the rest of you; the information you gain in the rest of your pilgrimage will guide your steps, confirm your call, and grant the peace that clarity provides.

This book does not cover every issue you should consider or explain all of the ramifications of missions, mission agencies, or missionary training. No single book, much less a single chapter, could attempt to do that. The primary concern here is to help you to be aware of, and begin to pray through, the pertinent issues as you explore ways to get to the mission field.

There are a number of practical issues to consider: How do you choose from the hundreds of mission agencies you will invest your time and energy and perhaps the rest of your life with? Some of them will pay you a salary while others require you to raise financial support from family, friends, and churches. Some focus on specific geographic regions and others target people groups. How does the location or people group to whom God is calling you become clear? Missionary training and missions education are essential to effective service, but how much is necessary and where can you get it? Considering these very practical issues will serve to guide you in understanding God's call and finding your place.

You should also consider theological and philosophical issues pertaining to your call. Missionary training and missions education guide you in answering many crucial theological and philosophical questions such as, What is the gospel?, or What is the goal of missions? These questions and many others await you on the mission field; you should know the answers to them before you get there. Exploring issues such as the Bible's responses to the challenge of pluralism and inclusivism is increasingly important. Or the question of whether missionaries should focus on social needs or preaching the gospel. The answers to questions such as these are stepping-stones along a path you know you must walk. You feel a holy restlessness that leads you on this journey and will not be at peace until you know its end. Marjorie Collins wrote,

> Many of you are seeking God's leading in your future ministry. You are earnestly desirous of allowing your talents, gifts and abilities to be used to their highest good in the cause of missions. You are looking for His positive direction to a Board, a field, a ministry, and a people to which you can give not only your best for the master, but also receive satisfaction from the ministry into which you enter. Lesser pursuits will result in frustration—no matter how high the position or how tempting the wages.[1]

CHOOSING A MISSIONS AGENCY

Those who are still struggling to know God's will should be encouraged to learn that the process of choosing the right missions agency, and even the appointment process itself, helps to discern and confirm the call. This process gives you the opportunity to talk to missionaries, agency directors, and even mission agency presidents to learn of their vision, theology, strategies, and methods. Choosing the right mission agency for you and your family is crucial. If your denomination has a sending agency, you must decide whether to apply for missionary service with them. If not, there are hundreds more, and each has its own unique strength and specialty. Sorting through the options can be bewildering and overwhelming. Resist the temptation to bypass the hard work of investigation. This choice is much like choosing a spouse—especially if you are considering career missions—because you will be conformed to its thinking and practices in many respects, you will spend a lifetime together, and your joy is largely dependent on a harmonious relationship. This choice may determine the length of your missions career in addition to your effectiveness and fulfillment. Gordon Olson reminds us, "Someone has well said that choice of a mission board is far more important than choice of a country."[2] Indeed, I have heard from candidates on several occasions that they felt led to work with a specific agency, not so much a country, language, or people group as yet, but they knew for certain that they were called to work with a certain agency.

Although a few mission agencies provide a salary for missionaries, the vast majority require that you raise your financial support. Some only require you to raise partial salary support, but most require full support to be raised by the missionary candidate. The prospect of raising support is daunting for many candidates. J. Hudson Taylor and China Inland Mission led the way in this model of missionary support. Many missionaries feel intimidated, mistakenly believing that they are beggars and asking strangers to part with their hard-earned money for their own personal gain. That is not the case at all! Rather, you are giving Christ's church an opportunity to invest in kingdom advance. Don Hillis explains, "The missionary of the Cross does not accept the gifts of God's people as handouts for his personal well-being. He is a representative of God's work. That work does not go on without God's servants doing it, and they cannot do it without support."[3] A healthier view of support-raising is to remember that you are recruiting a cadre of believers who will pray for you, visit you on the field, welcome you when you come home, and be advocates for missions, in addition to their monthly support of your ministry. You are raising a team of people who will serve as *senders* with you as the *goer* in your missionary endeavors. Hillis continues, "There is little in the life of the Christian worker that will do more to promote a long-time interest in both giving and intercession on the part of the home church than personal relationship."[4]

As you see God slowly but surely putting your financial support in place, your sense of call grows deeper. It is both humbling and affirming to realize that God stirs the hearts of His people to provide your financial needs. A. T. Houghton states, "You may be sure that, if God has called you, He will also supply your financial need to enable you to be fully equipped for His service. This dependence upon God and trust in Him for the supply of your need will be further assets in your preparation, and will greatly strengthen your faith, as you prove God's faithfulness."[5] Hillis agrees, "When the missionary candidate looks on the raising of his support as an opportunity to prove his faith, to inform fellow Christians of God's work, to inspire them to invest in things of eternal consequence, and to encourage them in their intercession for him and the work of the Lord, then his deputation is no longer a mountain but a ministry."[6]

The mission agencies that provide full salaries and require no support raising are few. Denominations, large churches, and some relief agencies dominate the list of these options. At first glance, the full-support model certainly seems much more attractive to candidates than the support-raising model. However, there is a trade-off and you should bear in mind two significant considerations. First, the full-salary support model normally requires an appointment process that is much more thorough than you experience when you raise your own support. Second, the support-raising model increases the level of accountability with the local church.

The International Mission Board (IMB) of the Southern Baptist Convention (SBC) provides a full-salary package for its missionaries and has a demanding appointment process. Historically, the IMB (formerly Foreign Mission Board) has required a level of thoroughness unknown in other agencies. For instance, Louis Cobbs reports on the SBC appointment process in the 1930s and

1940s, "The Foreign Mission Board was the first in the nation known to require missionary candidates to have a psychiatric examination as a part of the appointment process. . . . During their three-day visit in a psychiatric hospital, they wrote their personal histories and had a complete medical, neurological, and psychiatric appraisal."[7] Of course, this thorough appointment process (which no longer requires a stay in a psychiatric hospital!) springs from the profound sense of fiduciary responsibility and stewardship that the IMB believes it owes the churches of the SBC.

Mission agencies have historically employed many instruments and examinations to determine fitness for service. Ted Ward writes, "Across the past 200 years, and especially as mission agencies have come to be seen more in their managerial and technological functions, screening of potential personnel has become much more pervasive. The difficulty of assessing spiritual gifts and the pressure to deploy younger missionaries have caused a shift from literal biblical criteria in favor of measurable competencies and traits."[8]

In the IMB appointment process, the first question that candidate consultants explore with potential candidates is their sense of the missionary call. In a recent message to potential candidates, one consultant declared that they were looking for people who *know* that they are called. All candidates, i.e., both spouses, must articulate a missionary call in order to serve with the IMB. Cobbs reports, "Four elements of call were identified: (1) God's call to salvation; (2) God's call to an awareness of gifts and talents He has given; (3) God's call as an inward compulsion; and (4) God's call which involves other Christians—one's pastor, fellow Christians, church, and mission board."[9] Cobbs continues, "An assurance of God's calling and leadership was considered vital to one's being able to persevere and serve effectively overseas."[10]

The requirement of a missionary call is one of the more controversial elements of the appointment process since there is no "chapter and verse" in the Bible that defines or demands it. However, agencies like the IMB have found through experience with thousands of missionaries that the requirement of a missionary call is one of the keys to missionaries staying on the field when times get tough. Articulating a missionary call, defending it before family and churches, and persevering through a long appointment process results in a profound sense of call that will sustain you through the difficult days of language study, international living, and proclaiming Christ in a place where most of the people do not want you to be.

There is a second issue to consider when weighing the full-salary model against the support-raising model. When you raise your own support, your supporters provide much of your spiritual accountability. Yes, the faith mission agency with whom you relate will provide oversight as well. However, there is a built-in "check and balance system" when your support is provided by individuals and churches who know you and stay abreast of what you are doing. Full-salaried positions often involve detailed job assignments with micro-managers over all aspects of your work. Conversely, when you raise your own support your job description may be as broad and fluid as "whatever the Lord leads you to do." Some missionaries love the structure of a job assignment, having a supervisor, and being part of a team. Others prefer the freedom to follow God's leading on the field just as they followed Him to get there. Our family has experienced both models; each one has its own strengths and weaknesses. You know yourself and your family best. Would you prefer the structure of the salaried model or the freedom that comes with the faith model?

Security Issues

Other mission agency considerations often relate to practical issues such as strategy and methodologies. For instance, many agencies are utilizing platforms to gain entrance to "creative access" countries. These countries tightly control visas for legal residence and only allow people to enter who bring a needed skill valued by the government. Since gospel-hostile governments do not grant

Christian missionaries such visas, the Christian worker must obtain a visa by utilizing a platform such as business consultant, computer consultant, English teacher, or some other needed skill. Affirming the benefits of platforms, Barnett says, "Creative-access platforms are viable, God-given means for providing missions workers the opportunity and relational basis for effectively completing their main objective or mission. Far from a 'cover' for covert activities, platforms are a basis for living among, interacting with and communicating the gospel to those around us with a sense of integrity."[11]

Once in the country, missionaries are able to engage in other activities as time and freedom allow. However, many missionaries are uncomfortable with the platform arrangement. Many have asked what they will say to the young convert who learns during the discipleship process that his new Christian friend is really a missionary who came to target him and not a business consultant at all. More than one new convert has wondered what else the Christian has misrepresented. Some missionaries wonder whether the use of platforms results in them building their ministries on a fabrication instead of the truth.

Creative access missionaries live international lives of intrigue and excitement. That is extremely attractive to many candidates; to go where no one has gone before and do ministry against the wishes of gospel-hating rulers seems very much like the book of Acts. These missionaries use encryption software programs to protect the contents of their emails, use code language when writing home (like "yarping" to Dad instead of praying to the Father), and live life undercover. It can be very exciting, but it can also be very draining. This life is not for everyone. God has wired some of you to live in places where you can preach, teach, evangelize, and disciple openly. Shakespeare said it well, "To thine own self be true." You know how God has made you and your family. Platforms are means of creative access into countries that are otherwise closed to the gospel. Yet, they require a way of life that not everyone is called to live.

Choosing a Team

Another step on your journey to the field is to get to know your team. Many mission agencies work in teams that often include veteran missionaries, and increasingly, national believers. When you join an existing team on the mission field, it is a lot like your family: you don't get to choose who you get! It is critical that you take the time and expend whatever efforts or funds necessary to get to know your team before you sign on. I recently counseled a young couple on the field who arrived to serve in their chosen country with eyes and hearts wide open. They poured their lives into the work. However, they were in a very dysfunctional team situation and found that a disgruntled team member was undermining their work. After painfully working and praying through this agonizing experience, this couple asked me to warn all candidates to make sure that they get to know their team members before they accept an assignment—even if they must invest the money to go on a mission trip to meet them on the field. That advice may sound a little frightening and over the top to you, but a favorite strategy of the enemy has always been to divide and conquer. Email them, call them, and travel to visit them. Read their prayer letters and write them letters. Get to know your team and make sure both you and they think you are a good fit.

You need to learn what they are doing and whether you will fit in. For instance, some missionaries who work in Muslim countries will call themselves Muslims since the word simply means "one who submits." They use the word Allah to refer to God since that is God's name in their language. Others use the Koran to evangelize since it speaks well of Jesus in certain passages. Yet, many missionaries experience an aversion to this strategy that borders on a visceral response—they get sick about it! Whether or not this is a viable strategy built on sound missiology is not the point under consideration. The point here is that the time to investigate your team's strategy is not when you arrive as a new missionary and they say to you, "Here's your Koran, Muslim brother. You're a missionary; Go

tell others of Allah!" The intra-team grief, anguish, and dishar-
mony that your disagreement and angst will cause are not fair to
your team. More importantly, the stress and aggravation will overwhelm you and your family; and when added to your burgeoning
culture shock, it will probably make the adjustment too great to
withstand.

The possibilities for team disagreement are, unfortunately,
endless. Missions writers have stated and restated for decades that
the primary source of missionary stress and frustration is other
missionaries. You can avoid much of this confusion by getting to
know your team before you join it. Theologically conservative missionaries would be wise to find out whether the team—especially
the team leader—is liberal or moderate. Missionaries who are
Calvinists and emphasize the sovereignty of God would suffer, and
cause others to suffer, if placed on a team of Arminian missionaries who stress the responsibility of man. Of course, people do not
always hold doctrinal differences to the extremes and teams can
function in healthy relationships when team members agree to dis-
agree, and prize unity and brotherly love as Christ commanded.
Still, becoming aware of these differences and their degrees of
severity can help the candidate know whether he should join the
team. At the very least, he can recognize potential tension points
and avoid team strife. Some teams emphasize meeting the physical
needs of the national population while others stress proclaiming
the gospel. The wise missionary candidate will learn what he or she
believes about these issues and find out what the potential team
believes in order to avoid friction and pain. A great place to start is
David Hesselgrave's *Paradigms in Conflict*, where he discusses both
sides of ten different issues that regularly cause friction in the mission family. No matter what it costs, get to know your team!

MISSIONARY TRAINING

Why do you need missionary training? That takes time. One-
third of the world's population has never heard the gospel and

50,000 of these people are dying daily. It seems that the time is now and the call is urgent! After all, you do not need to go through Navy SEAL training before you can save a drowning child in a pool, and you do not need a seminary degree to share a tract. This argument and many like it reverberate in the halls of missions conferences. The well-intentioned sound bites seek to spur young people to think about the needs of the world and go to the nations without delay. Missions speakers and agency administrators have seen young people walk forward, sign a card, and commit to international missions. Yet, unfortunately, in college, they often incur debt that precludes their deployment. Other times, they fall in love and marry someone not called and committed, or they fall in love with the American dream of a house with a picket fence, 2.5 kids, a dog, and a new car. The speakers and administrators want to get young people to the field sooner, rather than later, to avoid the risk of losing these volunteers. However, major problems arise when they arrive on the field without thorough training.

I recently heard a missions speaker say to an audience of candidates, "You new missionaries will be forming the theology of this people group." He was challenging them to go to a field where some people had accepted Christ, but where there were no discipled believers. He was right and his statement was only the tip of the iceberg. The new missionaries will write theology and doctrine on the hearts of the people. However, many of the candidates were not yet sure what they themselves believed about many doctrinal issues, and many would soon be going "toe-to-toe" with Muslim imams, skeptics, atheists, New Agers, Hindu priests, and cult followers.

Missionaries must be prepared to represent Christ and His church in settings where often there is no church. They will also find it necessary at times to reprove and correct heretical church leaders. Church-planting missionaries must be able to distinguish between a Bible study and a new church. What are the biblical qualifications of a church or a pastor, and who should administer the Lord's Supper and baptism? Missionaries must often address polygamy in cultures where it has ruled for centuries or clearly explain the Trinity so detractors understand that they are not worshiping multiple gods. These weighty issues require a weighty preparation. My college alma mater took its motto from Mark 10:45: "For even the Son of Man came not to be served but to serve." My alma mater for my doctoral work proclaims the motto, "A mind for truth, a heart for God." All are essential—hands, feet, head, and heart. Hands that are ready to serve and feet that are ready to go are commendable, but the head and heart must also be prepared.

The preparation that a missionary candidate needs goes beyond what is necessary to share a gospel tract. A medical missionary who is a trained surgeon may spend most days in activities that do not require all of his years of training and surgical residency. Sometimes he conducts a wellness clinic, gives out worm pills, or immunizes and puts on Band-Aids. Yet, on the days that surgical skill is required, the zeal and burden to get to the field would be no substitute for the years he spent in school. No one would hire a lawyer or engineer who was eager to help but only had rudimentary knowledge of his field. Preparation is not wasted time; it is essential for effective service. Oswald Chambers reminds us that not only is preparation important, it should never end: "It is easy to imagine that we will get to a place where we are complete and ready, but preparation is not suddenly accomplished, it is a process steadily maintained."[12]

In fact, missionary training and the education process confirm the missionary call in many cases. Students often come to seminary to study missions because a mission trip or a missions course in their local church stirred them to know more. Others come to seminary because they know that God is calling them to take the next step in their Christian life, that He is calling them to some kind of ministry. While they are not yet sure exactly what that means, they know that a call to ministry is a call to prepare. As the semesters pass, they hear the heartbeat of missions professors, go on mission trips with fellow students, listen to the testimonies of the missionaries who speak in chapel, read missionary biographies, and wrestle with God's call on their lives. God uses all of these elements to focus their calling and guide them to the best pathway for their lives. To cite Psalm 32:8, "The LORD says, 'I will guide you along the best pathway for your life. I will advise you and watch over you.'" (NLT)

CULTURAL ISSUES

In the same way that knowing about the sharp edges of team members' personalities can assist you in avoiding tension on the field, so can knowledge of the culture to which God has called you. You should not run from God's leading to join a team simply because there are imperfect people on it. Rather than escape, you should use that awareness to promote harmony. Likewise, knowledge of cultural challenges that await you should not guide you to reject the hard places and opt for the soft ones. However, "forewarned is forearmed," and this knowledge should help you to anticipate and reduce the number and impact of cultural incidents that wear away your patience and sanity.

Every culture uses language for two reasons. One is to communicate information and the other is to maintain relationships. The culture of the United States uses language in this order of priority. Relational, face-to-face cultures of the group-oriented societies of the world operate with an opposite order. Our culture of direct communicators expects honest answers to questions; in fact, our society depends on it. But indirect communication cultures answer with what you want to hear in order to appease and avoid the awkwardness that saying no to a request might cause. The resulting confusion makes the North American missionary seem rude and demanding at times, while he thinks that people in the new culture are liars who are incapable of telling the truth.

United States culture values privacy and one's personal rights. Yet, many cultures of the world consider this perspective selfish and cold. We raise our children to respect other people and be on time for appointments. Businesspeople in the Western world often play power games in our culture by keeping people waiting. However, other cultures believe that clock time is not as important as the event and sensitivity to the feelings of the people involved in the event. Sometimes tension occurs when a task-oriented, list-making missionary is leading a team that includes nationals from a culture that is more person-oriented. The task at hand eclipses all other considerations in the missionary's priorities; he cannot understand why his workers are playing soccer outside when they need to be finishing the project. Other potential sources of tension are different uses of space, eye contact, gestures, and nuances of daily interaction that do not carry the same meaning from one culture to the next.

The missionary candidate should not seek to understand his own culture and the cultural tendencies of potential target cultures so as to avoid the hard places and choose an easy fit; nor should he use the information to justify not going where God is calling. Awareness of cultural differences simply allows the new missionary to anticipate where the tension points will be. With this knowledge, he can pray for more grace when entering situations that he knows will be especially stressful and repeat the intercultural axiom, "It's not wrong, it's not stupid, it's just different!"

CONCLUSION

AN UNDERSTANDING that God is calling you to take a step toward the nations will lead to subsequent steps: mission agencies, missiological issues, team dynamics, cultural differences, and training options. Training in a theological seminary is a rich and rewarding experience. Seminary training is the most thorough, deep, and exhaustive pre-field preparation for missions, but it is not an option available to everyone. There are other options available for your preparation such as online courses, Bible colleges, and missionary training organizations. Of course, there is always the self-education of reading books on missions history, missionary biographies, cultural anthropology, and missiology, as well as interviewing missionaries about their experiences.

The missionary message is the gospel of Jesus Christ, once for all delivered to the saints. It is Good News in four parts: God is holy, Man is sinful, Jesus is the answer, and you must repent and be born again. The message is so simple. Yet, communicating these four truths to the cultures of the world is remarkably complex. You must learn the languages, live in the cultures, and befriend the nationals in order to gain a hearing and share the saving gospel message in culturally appropriate ways—ways that they can hear and understand. There is no other gospel. There are no relaxed rules for the hard places and the gospel message is essential for salvation.

The crucial choices of which mission agency is for you, and then the team considerations, are much like choosing your lifemate. An English proverb quips, "Marry in haste, repent in leisure." We may also apply this proverb to the missionary who rushes to the field with little or no knowledge of the people with whom he will live and work or little understanding of important biblical and theological issues. It is essential to choose your agency and team wisely. Prepare yourself with as many missionary skills and as much education as you can get. Your people deserve the efforts you expend in your preparation. The purity of the church and the soundness of their doctrine will flow from your teaching among them. Research the target culture and learn as much as you can before you get on the plane to go. This learning process itself will deepen your love for them and strengthen your sense of the missionary call.

HINDRANCES TO GETTING TO THE FIELD

THERE ARE TWO VERY simple biblical truths that relate to world missions: the world must hear the gospel and Christ has charged us to take it to them. Why then have the nations not yet heard the gospel after two thousand years? It is not because God has not provided sufficient numbers of Christians, or called sufficient numbers of us into missions. God calls many more than actually go. Many Christians testify to wondering about a missionary call at some point in their life but that subsequent life choices closed that door to them, or at least rendered it a very inconvenient option to consider. Isobel Kuhn, missionary to China and Thailand, addressed this concern when reflecting on a tribe that had recently asked for someone to come and teach them about Christianity.

> Ten years they have waited. Do you think that when they called
> for gospel messengers, God did not respond? It could not be.
> He gave His most precious Son that all might know and receive

eternal life. I think that man did not respond. It costs something to leave loved ones and the comforts of civilization. I believe that in each generation God has called enough men and
women to evangelise all the yet unreached tribes of the earth.
Why do I believe that? Because everywhere I go, I constantly
meet with men and women who say to me, 'When I was young I
wanted to be a missionary, but I got married instead.' Or, 'My
parents dissuaded me,' or some such thing. No it is not God
who does not call. It is man who will not respond.[1]

In fact, these same "hindrances" continue, and we often invent
or imagine others as well. Such hindrances allow us to turn away
from the world's need for Christ and to our own desires with a
clear conscience.

However, not every hindrance is imagined or even welcomed.
Some hindrances that bar, or temporarily frustrate, missionaries
from fulfilling their call are both significant and beyond their control. The life of a missionary is challenging and requires men and
women who are not only willing, but also fit and prepared. Missions historian Stephen Neill said, "Christian missionary work is
the most difficult thing in the world."[2] While we may invent and
imagine some hindrances, others are very real. But you can avoid
many of them before they hinder your missionary career. Other
kinds of hindrances can only be resolved by the hand of God.
There is great peace in remembering that He is sovereign and the
work of missions is His work. He can do in, to, and through us all
His holy will. Oswald Chambers expressed, "If a man or woman is
called of God, it doesn't matter how difficult the circumstances
may be. God orchestrates every force at work for His purpose in
the end."[3]

Therefore, discerning the will of God and your place in missions is crucial. If you are sure that He is calling, you can be sure
that He will also remove the barriers that would preclude your service, in His perfect timing. Rest in that. Even though Jim Elliot was

a fervent missions mobilizer, he counseled his friend Pete Fleming, who was eventually martyred with him, to consider the hindrances: "I have no word for you re: Ecuador. I would certainly be glad if God persuaded you to go with me. But He must persuade you. How shall they preach except they be sent? If the Harvest-Chief does not move you, I hope you remain at home. There are too many walls to leap over not to be fully persuaded of God's will."[4]

In this chapter, we will consider seven categories of hindrances to fulfilling the missionary call, and what you can do about them.

PHYSICAL

Mission agencies require candidates to be in good physical condition. While some agencies simply ask for a doctor's statement verifying that you are in good health, others require very thorough physical examinations, a complete blood CBC, X-rays, family medical history, and a psychological evaluation. Many missionary candidates find these tests intrusive and unnecessary. They wonder what possible difference it makes that their cholesterol is a few points too high.

Remember that missionaries often must serve in remote areas of the world, cut off from the advanced medical care that is available to most of the developed world. The missionary himself may be the only "doctor" for his or her family for many months at a time. Latent medical problems often surface due to the stress of missionary living or repeated bouts of GI problems caused by parasites or amoebas. Candidates argue that they have always easily managed minor medical conditions with regular checkups, over-the-counter medications, and watching what they eat. On the mission field, these conveniences and options are often not possible.

In addition, missionaries should be in good physical condition because the stress of international travel and living requires stamina. Missionaries who must live in hot, humid jungles with no balanced diet, no consistently dry shelter, and that hostile environment's constant threat of infection from the smallest cut, find that health can deteriorate quickly. Others who had only a slight asthma condition at home in the United States, find great difficulty living in a country where farmers burn off the fields, covering the region in heavy smoke and ash twice a year for weeks on end. Even those in very good physical condition often find living at altitudes of 10,000 to 15,000 feet above sea level taxing to their health. Missionary candidates who are excessively overweight find many circumstances too difficult for effective service and spend much of their time simply recuperating from daily life.

For these reasons, and a host of others too numerous to list, mission agencies care about a candidate's physical condition. Revealing all past illnesses and sharing your family history will help them to help you. Physical hindrances are real and sometimes preclude missionary service—at least in the place that you had planned to go. Thus, considering your health and the rigors of living in the various locations available to you can be one more way that God may guide you to know and do His will.

Craig Storti stresses that issues of culture shock are further complicated by the "country shock" of living in environments of extreme temperatures, altitudes, or landscapes that are very different from our home.[5] If your plan is to serve among the Aymara at 14,000 feet above sea level in the Bolivian altiplano, and the doctor discovers a medical condition that cautions against this move, you might choose a lower altitude location. I know missionaries who chose a specific city due to their health or a family member's who in this indirect way found the joy of their hearts and the perfect will of God. However, some candidates without this flexible perspective are unwilling to serve in a place that they themselves have not chosen. But as Henry Jessup wrote, "No one should go who is unwilling to go anywhere. There should be complete self-surrender."[6]

Candidates can avoid the frustration of many physical hindrances by maintaining good health and weight. Through proper diet and exercise, strive to be ready to serve anywhere and anytime that God chooses. In this way, candidates resemble a player on the sideline waiting for the coach's signal to send him or her into the game—ready, willing, and eager to go. The sad truth is that one-third of adults in the United States between 20 and 74 years of age are obese. Diabetes is also on the rise, partially due to U.S. citizens' increasing girth.[7] Missionary candidates are sometimes hindered from service due to obesity, lack of aerobic fitness, or the consequences of a poor diet. These things we can control. Always be ready for the Lord to call your name and send you into the world.

EMOTIONAL

Emotional and psychological hindrances can also keep a candidate from effective service. The stress of international living coupled with culture shock can shake you to your core and can make you question your faith, if not your sanity. Emotional and psychological stress can incite a dislike and distrust for the very nationals that you came to reach. Sometimes an issue from your past that you thought you had addressed and forgotten blindsides you and erupts through the layers of rationalization with which you had covered it with in the United States.

As with physical hindrances, emotional dysfunction can remain hidden and covered over in the comfort and familiarity of your US lifestyle. David Mays writes,

> Dysfunctional backgrounds must be overcome. Those who have struggled with abuse, addiction, broken families and relationship issues carry additional baggage that tends to surface under the pressures of cross-cultural conditions and spiritual challenges. Our large spaces and independent lifestyles allow us to avoid people with whom we have problems. Such issues are often not so easily resolved overseas.[8]

Children who are abused often develop survival and coping skills that are not healthy and continue to struggle with those behaviors into adulthood. Insecurities, fears, and anxieties that are soothed with food, friends, or busyness in the habits of life in the United States cannot be dismissed so easily in a new and unfamiliar environment.

Along similar lines, depression can also be debilitating and a great hindrance to service. Of course, everyone gets the blues from time to time. Some of the brightest lights in the sky of Christian heroes suffered depression from time to time—King David and Elijah come to mind from the Bible along with Martin Luther and Charles Spurgeon from Christian history. Missionaries often suffer from homesickness, discouragement, and loneliness, which are to be expected. However, a clinical depression that grows into a pit of despair is not only debilitating but also dangerous, and intervention may be required. A proper assessment during the appointment process can be a wonderful blessing, not only to avoid such a meltdown on the field, but also to achieve health wherever you live.

Fears and worry are common to every believer. God knows that our sinful tendencies lead us to worry and anxiety, so the Bible is replete with admonitions not to fear or worry. Paul even gives specific guidance for having the peace of God (Philippians 4:4–9). The truth is, humanly speaking, there is a lot to be afraid of on the mission field. C. S. Lewis wrote that we live in a dangerous world;[9] nowhere is this more true than on the mission field. Most of the people do not want you there, the dominant religion surely does not want you there, and the Enemy does not want you there. There are diseases present for which your body has not built up immunity; there are wars, and often a rampant hatred of all things and people from the United States. Humanly speaking, you should be scared to death; but, then again, you already are dead, aren't you? "I have been crucified with Christ. It is no longer I who live, but Christ who lives in me. And the life I now live in the flesh I live by faith in the Son of God, who loved me and gave himself for me" (Galatians 2:20). Remember, the One who gave us our orders is sovereign and He loves you with a love you cannot fathom.

Elisabeth Elliot certainly had cause for fear as she, her young daughter, and Rachel Saint entered the tribal village of the men who had killed her husband and his four friends. Yet, she writes, "There is no need for faith where there is no consciousness of an element of risk. Faith, to be worthy of the name, must embrace doubt. In our going into Auca territory there were risks aplenty, so far as we knew. There was also the ground of our faith, the Word of Him who is called the 'Pioneer and Perfecter of our faith.'"[10] "It is the LORD who goes before you. He will be with you; he will not leave you or forsake you. Do not fear or be dismayed" (Deuteronomy 31:8).

SPIRITUAL

Every Christian should be in the pursuit of holiness. Yet, some pursue more diligently than others, and missionaries are no exception. Of course, the spiritual health of a missionary is important for his or her personal sanctification and growth in grace, but especially because the missionary sets the spiritual tone for the disciples on the field. In many places of the world, the only thing that the church members know of Christ and the Bible is what the missionary is, says, and does. There is no room for "glory-bound glory hounds." These types are the proverbial "bulls in a china shop" and they cause great damage to the work, other missionaries, and the cause of Christ among tender new believers. Pride and arrogance are distasteful among discipled believers in a strong Christian church, but they can be damaging for generations to come among young believers who are modeling their Christian lives after the patterns they see in the missionaries who teach them. Selfish ambition and friction can be unintentionally taught by Christian workers who have forgotten that godliness, love, and compassion should characterize our lives.

We often gloss over, rationalize, or excuse our besetting sins when confessing during our daily quiet-time devotions, especially when these sins are hidden, or even "acceptable" in United States culture. However, on the mission field everyone is watching you to see what a Christian is and how one behaves. You cannot relegate a biblical lifestyle to the realm of abstract debate as you live out your life before the nationals. All they will know about Jesus is what they learn from you. George Murray wrote, "Missionaries who take Christ's message to unreached peoples enter directly into Satan's territory. The enemy likes nothing better than to have missionaries fall into sin to nullify their witness."[11] The spiritual health of a missionary is more important than his or her physical health because a solid Christian testimony may give glory to Christ in ways that nothing else can. However, a missionary who backslides into carnality or selfishness works the opposite and hinders the advance of the gospel.

It is often more difficult to pursue holiness on the mission field. The combination of culture shock, country shock, rejection, and loneliness lives in the shadows of very little Christian fellowship, corporate worship, or friends to hold you accountable in your Christian walk. One of the reasons that Internet pornography addiction is on the rise is because it is a sin one can commit alone, without witnesses . . . in secret. Imagine living alone in another country. In an article dealing with missionaries' temptations, Murray said,

> Missionaries are usually far from home, far from those who know them, far from a Christian community. If they lose their temper or cheat a little bit, no one they know will ever find out, and no local Christians will be scandalized, because there aren't any. There is no local church, no believers, no Bible studies, no prayer meetings, not even Christian radio. . . . The missionary finds himself alone across enemy lines. Sin's attraction is strong, and there is no one nearby to help him stand against it. But we can overcome Satan, resist temptation, and not let sin dominate us, even on the mission field.[12]

A familiar proverb says your character is revealed by what you do when no one is watching. A. T. Houghton wrote, "Christian character is more than personality. It is not inherited or imbibed as other attributes may be. Its formation largely depends on the individual's determination to make use of outward circumstances and opportunities in its development."[13] As you grow in your Christian walk, you find that life is made up of choices. The choices you make not only grow out of your inner character, they shape your character. This symbiotic relationship reveals not only your true self, but who you are becoming.

A close relationship with God is essential for effective missionary service. A Christian's delight is in God and glorifying Him. In God's design, this delight in glorifying God also works to the missionary's benefit. The blessings that accompany living close to God are the necessary tools and building blocks for missionary work. You will not only be teaching and preaching, but also modeling what the believers need to learn—and they will learn more from what you are than what you say.

The communion with God that affects spiritual health results in the missionary's confidence in experiencing His leadership for life and ministry. Sensing God's guidance requires that you recognize His voice when you hear it. Aiden Gannett wrote, "Though subjective in nature, yet very really indeed the peace of God produced by the Spirit of God (Gal. 5:22) 'acts as umpire' in the heart to make definite the right decision in accord with the divine purpose. The means used by the Spirit in making each decision is the written Word (Col. 3:16; cf. Ps. 119:105)."[14] Simply knowing God's will provides clarity and boldness as nothing else can. Oswald Chambers made this connection when he declared, "We make calls out of our own spiritual consecration, but when we get right with God He brushes all these aside, and rivets us with a pain that is terrific to one thing we never dreamed of, and for one radiant flashing moment we see what He is after, and we say— 'Here am I, send me.' "[15]

RELATIONAL

People skills for healthy relationships are essential for missionaries. Imagine a shepherd saying that he would love his work if he just did not hate the smell of sheep! Missionaries must share the gospel and disciple believers, and this happens best in the context of personal relationships. Sometimes this requires you to love the unlovely and the unlovable. The missionary must have the skills to make friends easily and relate well in just about any situation. He or she is an ambassador for Christ—and it helps an ambassador to have the gift of diplomacy.

The missionary must also have good family relationships, both with family left behind and with the family members accompanying him to the field. You cannot leave behind family baggage by waving good-bye at the airport and fleeing to a far country; these problems will follow you and hinder your effectiveness. A missionary who cannot relate well to others will not be able to represent Christ. A missionary who does not get along with his or her spouse will not be able to hide that dysfunction on the field. The family is a model of the body of Christ. Relational skills are essential for working within a team, encouraging believers, and teaching about our relationship with our heavenly Father and Elder Brother.

FINANCIAL

I hope this does not come as a shock to you, but missionaries are not usually wealthy people. Those who have raised their support can tell you that it is a walk of faith to see the money come in each month. They can testify that although God is never late, He is seldom early. He provides what we need when we need it. That requires faith. Even those who receive full salaries for their monthly support are not paid handsomely.

The prospect of giving up a spacious, well-furnished home and moving to a developing nation where you may live on less than a tenth of your current income is a daunting challenge for some and hinders their acceptance of the missionary call. The financial considerations are certainly worthy of your attention, especially if you have children who are dependent upon you. However, God will not lead you where He will not provide for you.

One financial hindrance is the fruit of a college custom that is now virtually the norm in the United States—student loan debt. Personal debt is one of the primary hindrances to missionary service, and since the majority of missionary candidates are recently out of college, the principal reason for the debt is school loans. Students who must borrow for college and defer payments until graduation may owe $50,000 or more at the end of a four-year degree. No responsible missions agency will allow a young candidate to go to the field on a missionary salary to cover the debt service on such a large loan. The student often feels in bondage to this debt and guilty that it has become a hindrance to fulfilling his missionary call. In a recent school year, the National Center for Education Statistics reported that about one-third of all undergraduates took out student loans and on average graduated with almost $20,000 in student loan debt.[16]

Mortgages and car loans are usually viewed differently since candidates can sell them before deployment and repay the debt. However, some candidates lament that they used their house or car to leverage for more loan than they needed and now owe more than they could recover in a sale. Perhaps the housing market is in a slump and this precludes a sale, and therefore their missionary service on the field.

John Piper admonishes all Christians to live a wartime lifestyle.[17] This does not mean living below the poverty line. It means using money wisely. You may need a car, you certainly have to buy clothes and the necessities of life, but choose wisely. Spend money on what is necessary to win the nations. I have been finishing my basement to add a study and more living space for my family. After a couple of estimates from contractors, we decided that we should tackle the job ourselves to save money. I read books that explained how to do each step along the way, and then went as far as I could before researching the next step, and moving on. Along the way, I determined that some jobs were beyond my skill level and paid someone to do the job—so I could know my family would be safe from my electrical or plumbing efforts! I also had to buy some expensive tools to do the job. Well, they were expensive to me, anyway! I carefully weighed each purchase and based the decision on whether I would ever use the tool in the future. If this were a one-time, expensive tool, I paid a professional with the right tool to come do the job, but if I would use it many times in the future, I would buy it. Then, I shopped and compared before I bought a tool to make sure that it was the best quality for the best price. I did not buy anything I would not really need but I would gladly spend money when necessary (for the safety of my family or for the right tool for the job). We have just about finished the basement now and have done so at an unbelievable savings. Upon reflection, I am convinced that this is how we should live all of our lives for the advance of the kingdom and glory to Christ. Ask yourself, "Is this expense necessary; if so, is it the best way to spend this money?" Think of the funds that would be available for missions if every Christian lived that way.

Steer clear of debt. It quickly becomes bondage debt and you will not be free to serve the Lord in the way, time, and place He wants. Ironically, God's Word teaches us that it is a "debt" that admonishes us to live debt-free: "Owe no one anything, except to love each other, for the one who loves another has fulfilled the law" (Romans 13:8). Love for Christ and for the nations who need to hear compels us.

RAISING SUPPORT

The idea of raising your own financial support is often a hindrance that keeps many off the mission field. The specter of going into churches, speaking to missions committees and unfamiliar congregations, and asking them to give you money is overwhelming to many candidates. They say that they feel like unwelcome intruders who must march about from church to church to beg with their hat in their hand. They must raise support to furnish a home on the field, purchase a vehicle, and a host of other expenses such as travel to the field, monthly support, children's education, insurance, and retirement—and pray that it will continue the whole time they are overseas.

The work of missions is God's work. He is the One who calls us to do the work and provides everything we will need to do what He desires. In the same way that your missionary call fills you with inexpressible joy at the thought of serving Christ on the mission field, those with the gift of giving experience joy and fulfillment in exercising their gift on your behalf. God will enable you to speak and cast your vision so that you can raise the support you will need. Oswald Chambers wrote, "God does not ask us to do the things that are easy to us naturally; He only asks us to do the things we are perfectly fitted to do by His grace, and the cross will come along that line always."[18]

FAMILY CIRCUMSTANCES

Another category of hindrances and frustrations to fulfilling a missionary call is family circumstances. For instance, many agencies have set guidelines that preclude from service anyone who has ever divorced. Others will consider the couple or divorced singles on a case-by-case basis. Sometimes the rules are less stringent for those applying for shorter terms than lifetime, career appointments. After their first term, many of the couples who have shown a solid testimony and family stability are allowed to sign up for subsequent terms.

Most agencies appoint single people to missionary service, and missions history reflects that some of the most significant advances have been through singles—starting with the apostle Paul! Usually, singleness is a hindrance in the eyes of the candidate more than the agency. Many missionaries, like the apostle Paul, have found their singleness can be a benefit. Many have speculated that the reason the Huaorani[19] received Rachel Saint and Elisabeth Elliot without harming them was because single women posed no threat. Elisabeth Elliot wrote, "We foreign women were anomalies in every way, but perhaps the thing that aroused more curiosity among our neighbors than anything else about us was that we seemed to have no men."[20]

Having the gifts and calling to be a missionary without the gifts and calling to be single creates a challenging dilemma when you have not met your soul mate. The reasons this is challenging are many. When you go to the mission field single, you greatly reduce the possibility of meeting a potential mate, unless you marry a national there or another single missionary. If you meet someone and marry on the field, your agency must approve of your spouse or you must return home. In addition, many agencies have policies against dating on the field, so many single candidates feel that they are choosing either singleness and obedience to the call or disobedience to God and staying home to find a spouse. There is a lot of guilt among missionaries over these feelings of failure—usually false guilt. God has made you to be the person that you are and knows exactly what will complete you. Sometimes, a short term of one or two years on the field will teach you more about what God wants you to do than all the counselors in the world. Remember that God is not only sovereign over "either/or," He is also in charge of when and where.

In chapter 7, we saw that the spouse's shared sense of call is a key issue in both appointment and family life on the mission field. In addition to a mission agency's requirements for appointment, this shared call results in harmony and joy in the missionary home. The absence of it results in a major hindrance—of strife, tension, and ineffective ministry for the family on the field.

Missionary children are also a part of missionary families and their presence in a home can open many doors for effective service. Children open windows of witnessing opportunities and often make wary nationals lower their guard. Yet, having children can also, in one sense, be a hindrance to appointment. Some agencies will not appoint a couple with a new baby—they may consider the field you have chosen to be too dangerous an environment for one so tender. Other agencies will not appoint couples with teenage children. They have found through years of experience that teenagers are making so many adjustments as it is that the added burden of isolation and culture shock in a new country is too much. Therefore, they tell the parents to contact them again when the kids are in college.

Other considerations for missionary children concern their care and education. The medical care that children require may limit places of service. Someone must care for the young children during the day or while parents minister away from home. Their need for education must be met by leaving home and living in a boarding school, enrolling in an expensive international school if one is available, attending a national school, or home schooling. Missionary families are increasingly choosing the home schooling option for economic reasons. However, this normally limits the missionary activities of Mom solely to teaching the children, and that limitation may be frustrating to Mom or the mission agency.

God knew that you had children when He called you. His timing may be to wait, or His will may be to investigate other agencies or ministry location options. Elisabeth Elliot shared her own insights into this liberating truth,

> It was only gradually that I came to understand that some
> things are meant to be cherished, and not sacrificed. God was
> responsible for my parentage and my nationality and my up-
> bringing. He had called me, and He had called me by name,
> and He would not bypass what I was or the things that had
> made me what I was.[21]

DEALING WITH HINDRANCES
These are important considerations in the minds of many

mission agencies and they have policies to guide them. Consequently, they will be important to you too. Such policies that seem to hinder your service are not in place merely to protect the agency; they protect you and your family also.

It is disheartening to learn that a circumstance of your life, family, or past is a hindrance to your serving on the mission field in the way you had planned. However, the right attitude goes a long way in the persuasion of a mission agency's personnel department to consider other options that may be open to you. The hardest thing to hear is "no"; the second hardest is "wait." Yet, for the glory of God and the advance of His kingdom, we endure all things for the sake of those who have yet to hear.

Finally, remember that a hindrance to service may be just that—a hindrance; it is not necessarily an insurmountable barrier. There may be a way over it, under it, or around it. If a medical doctor advises against missionary service, seek to improve your health, lose weight if that is the problem, lower your cholesterol, and make the changes necessary to be fit for service. Perhaps the doctor cautioned against your appointment because your health would not stand the rigors of the location for which you applied. In that case, maybe another region would be suitable. If the hindrance to your service is debt, start paying it off with fervency. If you lack training, get it. If a divorce in your past bars you from career service with one agency, investigate the possibility of shorter terms, or even another agency. If your children are too young or too old, wait or look elsewhere. The point is that a hindrance is not a "no." You can avoid many hindrances by making intentional lifestyle choices that will preclude them. Other hindrances beyond your control may limit or redirect your expression of the missionary call and result in one of the ways the Lord guides us to His will. Some hindrances already exist in your life and cannot be avoided. Others can only be removed by divine intervention. He is able, and He can do more than we ask or imagine when we seek to live for His glory.

CHALLENGES ON THE FIELD

THERE IS A VERY GOOD reason that wise, godly leaders have said that missionaries are heroes; being a missionary in another culture and language in some of the far-flung places of the world can be incredibly difficult, frustrating, dangerous, and lonely work. To remain faithful in it requires a unique mix of talents, gifts, skills, and the enabling hand of God. In this chapter, we will discover some of the challenges you will encounter on the field to fulfilling your missionary call. These challenges make ministry—that would be difficult work under the best of situations—inconceivable apart from God's empowering grace. Raising such issues is not meant to discourage you, but to alert you to the potential potholes so that you can anticipate and avoid them.

CULTURE SHOCK
Culture shock is a bumpy road that every intercultural worker must negotiate. Seasoned travelers sometimes naively think that they will not really suffer it so much. However, while the peaks and

valleys of the experience may not be as extreme for some as for others, everyone goes through the cycle of adjustment. The shock often sneaks up on you and catches you when you least expect it.

After the long process of discerning God's will for your life and embracing a missionary call, you begin the appointment process or sharing your vision for missions to raise your support. As you complete each necessary step, you are more excited and eager as you anticipate arriving on the field to begin your ministry. At last, the day comes when you receive clearance to travel to the field. As you board the plane, knowing that thousands of prayers are finally beginning to find fulfillment, your excitement knows no bounds!

The first weeks in the country are like a honeymoon. You feel like you were born for this culture and that nothing could go wrong. We refer to this as the tourist stage since this is the deepest level of involvement that most travelers reach. All of the sights are new and beautiful and the colors are brilliant in the fields and village markets. You find that you cannot describe in letters home how the fragrances of the restaurants, fields of flowers, and bakeries perfume the air. The money is like the money of some board game—all different sizes and colors! The food, music, customs, and hospitality of your new home make you wonder why everyone hasn't moved here. Even the challenge of not speaking the language yet is more of a novelty than a bother. Enjoy this stage; it will only last a few weeks.

The next stage is the deep pit of the rejection period. This happens because everything that once was normal is now abnormal and you cannot function as you once did. No one speaks your language, which means you cannot either. The delicious fragrances that once enchanted you have become a stench. What happened? Did something change? The more you think about the food, the more it seems too bland—or too spicy—and you miss your mom's cooking. All of the beauty that you once saw is now an eyesore. You never really noticed the litter and graffiti before, but now it seems to be everywhere. You are constantly doing the math in your head to convert the local prices into "real money." The once-beautiful music is now a racket to your ears, and played much too loudly. You believe that the nationals are out to get you, take advantage of you in every transaction, and are thieves in waiting. What is happening, and why did you ever come here?

Telltale signs identify this rejection stage. There will be the smell of hamburgers cooking in the missionary home on a daily basis. The music heard there will be worship music from the home church. The television will be featuring a favorite DVD brought from home. The jeans, sneakers, and ball caps will all be from the United States. The T-shirt will have an American flag or a slogan in English. None of these things is wrong or earmarks of a failed missionary. Yet, when they begin to characterize and dominate his or her life, defining every single day, culture shock is usually at work.

The inability to speak the language results in frustration in daily life, like ordering a pizza or paying a utility bill. It also makes you paranoid. When two nationals are speaking their language and begin to giggle, you are sure that they are laughing at you. If you have just tried speaking in their language, they probably are! However, when your child is ill and you need to take him to the doctor, it is terrifying not to be able to speak the language. A friend of ours had recently arrived in a new country for language school. After someone from the language school dropped them off at the apartment that would be their home for the next year, their child suffered an epileptic-type seizure for the first time in her life. She was unconscious and they did not know what was wrong with her, the language, how the phones worked, or whom to call. He took his child in his arms and walked to the street. A passing motorist realized that he was in dire need of help, motioned for him to get in the car, and took him to an international hospital where English-speaking doctors could care for her. The inability to speak the language can be terrifying.

Crime is a reality all over this fallen world. When you are in a new country and going through culture shock, any crime seems personal.

What often makes it worse is when the more seasoned missionaries, forgetting how hard their own adjustment was, do not appreciate your hardships. I remember how angry I became during our early days of culture shock when a thief stole our kids' puppy out of our locked car while I ran into the post office to mail a letter. Some missionaries were amused that I would let such a little thing upset me. However, I took it personally; I fantasized about sting operations to catch the thief and get back at the one who had hurt my kids this way. Okay, so it was actually a minor thing as international crimes go and I was losing my grip on reality, but that is the whole point. When you are in culture shock and any crime occurs, you are angry, focused on the negative events, and unfairly characterize everyone you see on the streets as the potential thief. The nationals are not trusted and you begin to paint all of them with the same brush.

In order to compensate for your inability to traffic in educated, polite society of the new culture, you may begin to spend time with fellow English speakers. Perhaps you join the North American club or a country club, ostensibly because there is a pool there where your kids can swim or they can take tennis lessons. Soon, you are there several days of every week where you join with your expatriate friends making each other feel better by ridiculing the nationals. You begin to retell all the ethnic jokes you heard as a child, but now the nationals are the idiots in the story. Some candidates may find such unchristian behavior hard to understand or even believe. That shocked perspective is what adds to your shame and conviction when you find yourself joining in. You may begin to question your sanity or salvation.

You must be intentional about avoiding the sticky trap of expatriate exclusive friendships and get involved in the culture. In order to be salt and light in the world, you must be in the world. Sherwood Lingenfelter and Marvin Mayers have described the reason we persevere past this point in our adjustment.

Although we cannot reach perfection, we still can strive for the lesser goal of becoming incarnate in the culture of those we serve . . . we need to move from a position comfortable to us and our culture to a position approximating the goals of the culture to which we are sent. Wherever we serve, our objective should be to live in such a way that we respect, love, and share our very lives (including our priorities and goals) with those to whom we seek to minister.[1]

This is because, no matter how hard it gets, there is a joy that flows from obedience that overcomes the struggle. One missionary serving in Africa, recently wrote in a prayer letter,

I am sitting in a cybercafe in Conakry. There is no power so the cafe is running a generator. In fact, we only have six to twelve hours of electricity a day. Our refrigerator can barely keep stuff cold. There is no washing machine, so Billie does the laundry by hand. When it's dry, we have to let it sit for three days before we wear it so all the fly eggs hatch and die first instead of burrowing into our skin. We have no fans, even though it is quite hot and humid. We live in a house compound with an African couple, a short-term missionary from Canada, two dogs, two cats, three kittens, and a few toads and lizards. We must filter all water before we drink it. When we travel, we go by taxi. The taxis here carry six passengers at a time. All these things make life very interesting and a bit difficult at times. Still, we are enjoying ourselves because we are right where God wants us, doing what he wants us to do. The next time we are in the U.S., life will seem quite boring by comparison. What a joy it is to serve the Lord![2]

Paul Hiebert observes that another cause of this difficult time of cultural adjustment is role deprivation.[3] You may have been an important pastor, doctor, or teacher in your home culture and now you cannot even communicate at the level of a first-grader, much less fulfill your accustomed role in life. In addition, he notes that the comfortable routines of your life are gone. He describes these as the things you do in life without having to think about them: making a meal, driving to work, stopping at a store for milk, or ordering in a restaurant. In the new culture, life just seems very hard and it drains you dry. Frustrations are present that you never knew at home. Jim Elliot wrote of adjusting to life in the Ecuadorian jungle,

> The day was hot, and we had about a dozen men working on the foundation of the clinic building and clearing the forest directly behind. This afternoon a sudden tropical thundershower came up and blew the ridge off the roof line, turned the calendars over on the wall, and made a great mess of our shelves and papers with its wind. It only lasted about ten minutes, but it can give a man a lot to think about in that time. Screened windows leave one without anything to close when a storm comes.[4]

Little annoyances like these are easily dealt with one at a time. However, they usually come in waves that eventually wear down your cultural shock absorbers; from then on, you are metal on metal, crashing through the terrain of a new culture and wondering whether this will ever become easy.

This rejection stage can last from a few months to a couple of years. The length of time you spend in this deep valley depends greatly on how well you bond with the culture, learn the language, and make friends. Language skills are crucial for understanding cultural experiences and events. Once you learn the language, you can overhear two nationals laughing in their conversation and realize that it is in response to a joke's punch line and not about you. The comfort that comes with the ability to communicate easily also brings a greater sense of security.

Making friends in the culture is crucial. As you make friends, you can attend cultural events with your own personal guide and cultural interpreter. Learn to appreciate the food, music, humor, and rhythm of life. If the national foods seem very strange to you and your children, make a family rule that you will try one new national dish every week. This is manageable for almost anyone, and you will identify national foods you really like. The nationals will be happy and proud to see you enjoying their delicacies, and it will be less offensive when you avoid those you find less palatable. You can experience, and learn to appreciate, other aspects of the new culture in bite-sized chunks as well. The resulting benefit is that what was so *abnormal* to you just a few months ago will begin to be normal. In fact, you will find yourself preferring some of the cultural peculiarities to your own home culture.

Coming out of this valley of despair can take one of several routes; two are unhealthy and one is the ideal. The first unhealthy route is assimilation where some missionaries attempt to "go completely native." Some have tried to delete their past, attempt to forget English and their family back home, and totally embrace the new culture as if they had been born into it. This might sound like a healthy attitude, but it is not. God made you who you are and all of your life experiences are His gifts to you—even the bad ones are worked together for your good and His glory (Romans 8:28). Total suppression of your past is a recipe for psychological breakdown. Imagine getting married and attempting to delete your family of origin and all your previous life experiences; you would no longer be the person your spouse fell in love with. If you can embrace your past and the best of the new life, you will be better able to minister to the ones you came to evangelize and disciple, and stay healthy in the process.

The second unhealthy route is the other extreme of non-acceptance. Some missionaries never quite get used to the new culture, but only grudgingly acquiesce to the reality that they now live in it and cannot escape. They see no way out, because of the shame that would accompany resigning and returning home, or perhaps because their spouse loves the new country, or they do not wish to impede the family from fulfilling God's call. Missions to them is a life sentence. The result is that they constantly feel a culture-tension or culture-stress and they never accept the nationals as equals, never trust them, never sit next to them in a meeting, and never invite them into their home. Of course, they never say this aloud and often feel guilty for such an attitude. The effect on the family's missionary effectiveness is devastating. Culture-tension's actions speak much more loudly than its words.

On the other hand, the healthy way out of the pit of the rejection stage is cultural adaptation. This occurs when the new way of life that once seemed so abnormal begins to feel natural. In fact, it is hard to remember not soaking vegetables and fruits in bleach solution to make them safe to eat or buying meat neatly packaged in shrink-wrapped containers. Life in the new culture gets easier; it feels comfortable. The routines return; they are different, but a sense of normalcy is back and you feel good about life again. You cannot wait to visit with your friends back home and tell them all about this new life as you enjoy a few of your favorite things back home again.

Upon returning home you may be surprised to encounter a reverse culture shock. Most missionaries are anxious about living in a new country and culture, and they expect to have some culture shock. The whole time during their first term on the field, they daydream about how sweet it will be to go to their favorite fast-food restaurant, or enjoy the candy bars, cereal, Dr Pepper, or bacon that they may not have been able to get in the new country. They imagine enraptured friends listening to their every utterance as if they were Marco Polo returning from his travels. There is great shock upon finding that their friends' interest only lasts for a few polite conversations, and then they prefer to change the subject. They simply have no framework of reference for relating to the missionary's new culture. Most people want to talk about themselves, or at least something they know about.

You will also be shocked as you see the priorities and preferences of churches back home with a new perspective. How could they spend $10,000 to replace the upholstery on the pew cushions just so they will match the new carpet? Do they not know about the tens of thousands of children dying of starvation and the millions who need to hear the gospel? The sick feeling you get from the waste and wealth of churches back home lets you know that you have changed. It is true; you cannot go home again—not the same way you were when you left. You are increasingly a citizen of a third culture, not the one of your birth or your target culture, but some mixture of the two. You feel that you just do not have a home. This sense of displacement and loneliness is not expected and blindsides many returning or furloughing missionaries.

LANGUAGE LEARNING

Language school is a stressful experience for everyone in the family. It hits different family members in unique ways because of the differences in our needs and desires. For instance, husbands tend to need significance in their lives and wives tend to need security (I say "tend to" because both genders need both). However, total immersion language school threatens both spouses in both ways. The husband/father may feel his significance threatened when his wife picks up the language faster and scores better on language exams than he does—and when his kids are fluently chattering away with children in the neighborhood. It is hard for him to find significance when he cannot even ask for a glass of water in the new language, much less preach, teach, or share a simple plan of salvation. The wife/mother may feel her family's security is threatened when she cannot communicate with a neighbor, doctor, taxi driver, or police officer. This sense of helplessness is not imagined; it is very real. One positive result of this frustrating period of missionary life is that it throws us completely on the Lord for help and we live in constant dependence on Him.

The trials of language school are many, but well worth the effort. Some may advocate getting started in missions work with only minimal language skills, but these missionaries usually have poor communication abilities that hamper them all of their careers. In language school, the husband may have an unfair advantage over his wife if there are very young children in the family. In some cases, Mom must stay at home with the babies or toddlers and rely on a tutor. She may feel unfairly hampered in what God has called her to do. However, in other cases, Mom's interaction with domestic helpers or neighbors during the day gives her natural tutoring which results in fluency and ease with the language. No matter how you learn the language, make sure you do. Make friends and travel with nationals when you travel for work; ask them to critique your language skills; swallow your pride and learn to laugh at yourself. You will be a better speaker for Christ's sake as a result. The greatest missionaries had to begin learning the language sometime, and had to overcome the discouragement that all of us feel. Concerning his own feelings of inadequacy, envy, and frustration, Jim Elliot wrote in his journal,

> July 26—Marveled at my inner weakness yesterday. Felt miserably unworthy to be here as an "administrator of the mysteries of God." Strange that I should—evidently for life—be put to such close contact with Pete and Betty whom I feel are far my intellectual superiors.... They are both able to correct my grammar and pronunciation, and seem to be able to apply tense rules so much easier than I. Felt weepy and useless yesterday at noon, swept with waves of envy and defeated wonderings about such things.[5]

FAMILY LIFE

It is important to keep the lines of communication open in any family anywhere, but it is especially important on the field.

The dangers that exist in developing countries may require certain precautions and contingency plans that would not be necessary in the United States. Spending quality time with each other is essential—not only for harmony and encouragement, but also to ensure that a sense of unity and security is felt. The children need to know that Dad is available to them. The tyranny of the urgent drives the agenda for most ministers everywhere and this is true on the mission field as well. However, in the absence of the extended family and the support, comfort, and options of life in the United States, both parents need to spend time with the family. This is especially true if the missionary kids (MKs) in your family attend boarding school. During times of school breaks, Dad needs to rearrange his schedule in order to spend time with the family and maybe head to the beach.

Missionary families with children often find open doors and opportunities for ministry that others miss. Missionaries who come with children look less like spies or charlatans, which causes nationals to lower their guard. Blond-haired, blue-eyed, and light-skinned children in a nation of kids with dark hair, eyes, and skin are a source of amazement. They are like magnets to national mothers and children alike. Raising children on the field can be a great blessing and enhance your ministry, but also includes the challenge of educating them. MK schooling hits the family budget hard if they attend an international English-speaking school. You could choose a national school, but language is an issue—especially for older children. As we noted in chapter 9, home schooling is increasingly the educational method of choice.

Another major consideration for MKs is separation from family back home. As I watched our MKs interact with each other on the field, I often thought of the words of Jesus,

> Truly, I say to you, there is no one who has left house or brothers or sisters or mother or father or children or lands, for my sake and for the gospel, who will not receive a hundredfold now

in this time, houses and brothers and sisters and mothers and children and lands, with persecutions, and in the age to come eternal life. (Mark 10:29–30)

One of the ways we have seen the Lord fulfill this is that missionary families are virtual family for each other. MKs address other missionaries as aunts and uncles, and treat each other like cousins. While this is a great blessing to the missionary family, it is sometimes disconcerting to their extended families back in the States when the kids speak of aunts and uncles that no one at home knows! Many MKs feel closer to other missionary families than they do to their own blood relations in their parents' home country. Many times, these MKs were born on the mission field and the other missionaries kept the older children while Mom and Dad were at the hospital for the delivery, or they provided the care and support that their natural family would have back home.

These times of separation from extended biological family are not the only challenge of raising children on the field. MKs who grow up in another country learn the words to the national anthem of that country, say the pledge of allegiance to the flag of that country, and know the celebrities and sports heroes of that country, but may be totally ignorant of similar aspects of United States culture. This causes a kind of culture shock unique to MKs. When parents return home to the United States for furlough or stateside assignment, they think that the MKs are happy to go "home." They assume that they will enjoy being back "home" in the United States.

However, MKs are not sure where home is. One of the hardest questions for an MK to answer is, "Where are you from?" They may have been born in the United States, but they left when they were very young, and they may have lived in two or more countries since then. They often feel very much out of place in their parents' home country. This can cause a sense of guilt in MKs who secretly wish they could just stay with their friends while the parents go home. It is often said that they feel most comfortable on a plane between the two countries. Imagine these young people going into a church youth group in the United States for the first time as a teenager. They do not know the popular musicians, current movie stars, appropriate phrases among their age group, or even how to dress as expected. The peer pressure and even ridicule can be overwhelming for a teenage MK. However, MKs have skills that their age-group peers back in their parents' home culture do not share. I know MKs who traveled alone internationally while in their teenage years, and caught a taxi into Hong Kong to shop for the next school year's clothes while on a long layover.

The benefits of growing up as an MK and being a Third-Culture kid are phenomenal. MKs learn that happiness does not come from material possessions since their friends on the field are both happy and very poor by United States standards. Someone has said that you know you are an MK if you can speak three languages, but cannot spell in any of them, you see a machete and call it a lawn mower, you watch a National Geographic special and see someone you know, or go to the zoo and say, "Oh, those are so good to eat!" MKs are not just bilingual, or multilingual, they are bicultural and can move easily from one culture to another—and back again. Due to these cultural and linguistic skills, adult MKs who do not enter the ministry themselves often work as representatives for transnational corporations. MK life is challenging, but it produces some of the most remarkable people in the world. I know; two of them grew up in my home.

LACK OF PRIVACY

Western cultures have a strong sense of privacy, personal space, and personal rights. The collective, group-oriented cultures of the world do not understand or appreciate these values. The fact is that most of the mission fields of the world do not share the North American's sense of these "rights." For instance, in many cultures, it is perfectly appropriate to ask a woman her age or weight, or how much she paid for a dress. National neighbors may

feel free to borrow tools without asking or boldly request a ride to
a neighboring city. A national friend or colleague may arrive at
your home unannounced when traveling and expect to stay with
you—maybe for days at a time, if he has business where you live.

North Americans seem to think that privacy is a God-given
and inalienable right. When the foreign missionary goes down to
the river to bathe, nationals may gather to watch, and stare incredu-
lously, at the white skin of the missionary. Missionary families
who build walls in villages where walls are unknown are sending
the message that they do not wish to live like or with the nationals.
Elisabeth Elliot wrote of the stress that the lack of privacy causes
as she, daughter Valerie, and Rachel Saint lived among the Huaoranis in the jungles of Ecuador.

> Rachel was invited to share [a house] with Gikita, his wife
> Mankumu, and her children (his other wife, Umaenkiri, had a
> small house close by), and I was given a smaller house adjoining
> theirs. None of the houses was anything more than a roof. The
> total absence of walls, even though the houses were either
> joined together or within a few feet of one another, seemed to
> bother no one but me. I would have been glad, now and then, to
> be able to go into a room and close a door. . . . We had no
> choice in the way we lived. We were given an Auca house; we
> lived in it. It was no dream house. Besides the total lack of pri-
> vacy and cleanliness, there was the lack of protection from rain,
> insects, and even snakes. I began to contemplate making some
> improvements one night after finding a snake coiled near Va-
> lerie's head as she slept. There was no way of doing this, howev-
> er, without introducing new problems which we wanted to
> avoid at the time.[6]

Face-to-face, group-oriented cultures include everyone present. The concept of excluding certain people makes no sense to
them and is offensive. In addition, our culture stresses the personal

rights of individuals while others prefer to think of the needs and rights of the entire group.

SINGLE MISSIONARIES

A challenge faced by many single missionary candidates is whether to deploy to the mission field as a single. In addition to mission agency policies regarding, and regulating, dating and marriage on the field, there are other significant considerations. When I lead short-term teams, I always advise the singles to exercise great care with any potential relationships. Unfortunately, in some countries, the single nationals may believe that marriage to a United States citizen is their best, and sometimes only, hope for escape from poverty. They think that if they could only get to the United States, a wonderful life surely awaits them there. This motivation is rarely the road to marital bliss. If this is a warning for a two-week mission trip, it is a daily concern for single missionaries who live in the country. A friend who served as a single missionary in Africa said that the nationals always wanted to know why she was not married, and would boldly enter into this line of questioning with her. In their culture of arranged marriages, it was unheard of for a woman of marrying age to travel abroad as a single girl. The explanation that she had not met the man she felt led to marry was lost on them—it was just absolutely incredible to them! She finally discovered that when someone asked where her husband was, a culturally appropriate response was, "He is still in his father's house." That could mean that the arranged marriage partner was not yet of age, had not passed through initiation, or a host of other explanations, but it made sense to them.

Cross-cultural marriages also raise other issues. In some countries, the husband may be overbearing and demanding and this is considered appropriate behavior. The culture may expect the wife to be occasionally seen but rarely heard. While these extremes may take a milder form among believers, a young missionary should be aware of the cultural guidelines for marriage before he or she commits.

There will be a host of well-meaning national church members who want to "marry you off" to their brother, sister, cousin, or friend. Even in the best of circumstances, the single who dates and marries someone from another culture is committing to a lifetime of explaining—why things are funny, who famous North American personalities are, why we celebrate certain holidays, as well as all the pertinent cultural aspects of the national's background. Either the national or the missionary (or both) will live their life away from their family, and their children will grow up not knowing one family and its cultural heritage or the other—or both in some cases. Dating and marrying nationals on the field carries certain missionary career consequences, requires necessary explanations to the local church, and sometimes results in the loss of lifelong dreams or part of your self-identity.

No single answer to this dilemma covers every situation. Some singles sense a call to missions that surpasses all marriage considerations—especially if marriage would require resignation from their mission agency. They may feel, like the apostle Paul, that marriage would necessarily limit their usefulness, and that God gave them a call to missions before He allowed this opportunity to marry. Others believe that God has given them a call to international missions and has guided them to the field for a time, knowing the plan He had for them. They believe that God's plan was for them to go to the field and there meet the spouse He had prepared for them. They marry with a pure conscience and serve God in other ways the rest of their lives.

DISCOURAGEMENT AND DOUBTS

Spiritual warfare takes many forms as the Enemy battles against the advance of the Kingdom and the effectiveness of missionaries. One of the key weapons in his arsenal is discouragement. Learning the language can be extremely discouraging. I remember in my early missionary days getting in my car to drive home after preaching in churches on the field and repenting all the way home for how terrible my language skills were in the sermon. I felt like a bad person; it devastated my self-esteem, especially when teens in the congregation giggled or adults smiled at my mistakes. I felt that I would never learn, and it was so hard. I heard of a missionary who went to France for language school and became very discouraged when he could not learn the language. He found himself in a park debating inwardly about resigning and returning home. After a long time of prayer and introspection, he overheard two women talking on a bench behind him. He was overjoyed when he realized that he could actually understand what they were talking about. His realization grew into excitement, but then quickly dissipated and turned to disappointment when it dawned on him that they were speaking English!

We have recounted the difficulty of relationships with team members and nationals. Missionaries tend to be very strong-willed people. You go through all the steps to appointment, oftentimes you must raise all of your support, and you sell your belongings to move to the field. You arrive with a vision and zeal strengthened by the hardships you have undergone to make it that far. However, remember that the others on your team did that, too. They feel their vision just as strongly and it is rarely the same one. Cross-purposes do not make for harmonious relationships. When one feels a vision so strongly, he questions the spirituality of anyone who does not also embrace it. The mission team often ends up consisting of a bunch of people who are disgruntled and questioning each other's spirituality.

Oftentimes, nationals disappoint us. We think they are only interested in the money they think we have stuffed in every pocket. Perhaps the progress you believe you have made among the nationals evaporates when division breaks out among them. There may be a believer whom you are discipling and whom you thought was soundly converted, who turns back and abandons the faith. Or, a family in a gospel-hostile place accepts Christ, begins to share their new joy, and is martyred. Again, these disappointments rarely come one at a time but rather in waves.

Sometimes, the slow pace of the work is the source of disappointment. It seems the work takes a step forward but falls back two. It appears that no one wants to hear the message. The culture makes no sense and seems so chaotic. Family members fall ill and the Enemy reminds you that they would not be sick if you had stayed at home. This is your fault and you are hurting them for no reason since you see no fruit in your ministry. At other times, family members at home fall ill and you not only miss home, you feel guilty for not being there at a time of need.

The Enemy brings another weapon out of his arsenal when discouragement has done its work; it is the weapon of doubt. The questions that plague your thoughts give way to doubt about whether God actually called you. The Enemy will tell you that it was your own idea and sense of childhood adventure that made you risk your family on the field. Your doubts will cause you to question your own salvation, or God's power and love, or the truth of His Word when you see so many frustrations and so little fruit in your work. Mike Wakely wrote of these doubts,

> Even in those early years as an enthusiastic missionary, I faced constant questions and doubts about the task I had launched myself into. For every answer to prayer, my mind asked if it could be a coincidence. For every spiritual blessing, my mind wondered if this was an experience explainable by psychology. For every spiritual victory, I questioned why there was so much failure. . . . It is a struggle that knocks many people out of the race, unless they are equipped and prepared for it.[7]

The challenges on the field to fulfilling the missionary call are many. However, you have the calling, presence, power, and promises of God as you go forth. Yes, there are many difficulties, but there are also great rewards. I am haunted by the danger of living my life so that I will come to the end of it, look over my shoulder, and realize that I lived it in selfish comfort and convenience. Self-discipline yields eternal benefits and far outweighs the challenges of temporal obstacles. Paul challenged, "But I discipline my body and keep it under control, lest after preaching to others I myself should be disqualified" (I Corinthians 9:27).

11

MISSIONARY HEROES AND THE MISSIONARY CALL

WHEN DISCERNING GOD'S will for your life, it is wise to seek godly counsel. Imagine having the opportunity to sit down with David Brainerd, William Carey, Hudson Taylor, and other well-known missionary heroes of the past to ask their counsel, to learn all about their life, missions experiences, and missionary call. What a blessing that would be! By God's grace, we have that privilege through the writings they left behind and biographies written by those who knew them well. In our world of confusing voices and conflicting opinions, it would be refreshing to hear the clear clarion call of godly missionaries and missions-minded pastors speaking to us through the pages of history about the missionary call. Every generation has the blessing and duty to stand on the shoulders of those who have gone before, to learn from their failures, successes, and teachings. As we learn from the lives of some of the brighter lights in the missionary night sky, we stand on the shoulders of giants. Yet even there we see that the missionary call comes in a variety of ways, according to God's sovereign work in each individual life. But each story has something to teach us about missions, and especially the missionary call.

Some missionaries received their calling in mystical experiences. Susan Fitkin described her own when she wrote,

> I awoke trembling and greatly moved, and was wondering what it all meant, when I became conscious of the divine presence. It was like a person standing beside my bed, and in an audible voice saying solemnly: "Go ye into all the world, and preach the gospel to every creature!" I was astonished, for I was still an invalid, but I at once replied, "Oh, Lord, I will go, but you know how frail I am. You will have to take all the responsibility." He assured me that He would, and a great peace filled my soul. This was such a clear call that I never doubted it. This was a memorable occasion but it was only the human sanction to God's work. For, years before, He had definitely spoken His precious words to my heart: "Ye have not chosen me, but I have chosen you, and ordained you, that you should go and bring forth fruit," and has He not verified it again and again?[1]

Rachel Saint, lifelong missionary to the Aucas, also experienced what for her was an unmistakable missionary call, but to others is very mystical. On a transatlantic trip, as she was praying about an opportunity she had been offered to serve a wealthy woman who could have provided a comfortable life for her,

> Rachel was aware of something strange happening to her. It was as if she were not standing on the deck of the ship anymore but was instead standing in a jungle clearing, looking at a group of brown-skinned, half-naked people. The people beckoned for her to come to them. As quickly as the scene came, it left. . . . Rachel fell to her knees and closed her eyes, "God," she prayed, "I will give my whole life to You and go and be a missionary to those brown-skinned people if you want me to."[2]

Such experiences are remarkable, and seeing the fruit of the lives thus called, we hesitate to question them; but they are not the normative or usual manner of being called to missions. When potential missionaries read of such calls, they often doubt their own call, since it was not so mystical. Many remain at home awaiting a supernatural experience or mystical revelation of the will of God, determining that God has not yet called them.

It is encouraging to know that throughout history other well-known and respected missionaries spoke simply of a *sense of ought* that grew from an awareness of the great need, and this initiated and accompanied their missionary call. The need is not the call, as Thomas Hale reminds us, but it is often what God uses to get our attention to hear the call: "God's word, together with the urging of the Holy Spirit, constitutes the call. But the need certainly gives people an extra mental and emotional impetus for heeding the call."[3] Hale continues, "Being a missionary begins with being called. You don't choose to be a missionary; you're called to be one. The only choice is whether to obey."[4]

DIFFERING UNDERSTANDINGS OF THE MISSIONARY CALL

As we saw in chapter 4, others have emphasized the perspective that the Great Commission is the only call we need, and it falls to us to obey or not. The words of Ion Keith-Falconer have mobilized many to missions: "I have but one candle of life to burn, and I would rather burn it in a land filled with darkness than in a land flooded with lights."[5] It has been said that no one has the right to hear the gospel twice, while there remains someone who has not heard it once. Robert Savage, missionary to Latin America, lamented, "The command has been to 'go,' but we have stayed—in body, gifts, prayer, and influence. He has asked us to be witnesses unto the uttermost parts of the earth . . . but 99% of Christians have kept puttering around in the homeland."[6] William Booth, founder of the Salvation Army, exclaimed, "'*Not called!*' did you say? '*Not heard the call*,' I think you should say. Put your ear down to the Bible, and hear Him bid you go and pull sinners out of the fire of sin."[7] Some have placed great stress on the duty of every Christian to go unless clearly called to stay behind to send others. This going often required costly sacrifices and a martyr's death. When told by friends and loved ones that the sacrifice was too great, C. T. Studd once remarked, "If Jesus Christ be God, and died for me, then no sacrifice can be too great for me to make for him."[8] As he sailed from England to Africa in 1910, leaving behind his wife and four daughters, he wrote, "God has called me to go, and I will go. I will blaze the trail, though my grave may only be a stepping-stone that younger men may follow."[9] He remained fervent in missionary service in Africa until he died there in 1931.

The expectation that all should go to the mission field unless God directed otherwise saturated some church traditions. Louis Cobbs reports, "An article in the Southern Baptist Missionary journal in 1847 on 'The Duty of Candidates for the Ministry' implied that all ministers should go to the mission field unless they had a special call to remain at home. This was the view of the Student Volunteer Movement and was widely held by Baptists, including the first two secretaries of the Foreign Mission Board."[10]

Still others have emphasized an understanding of the call that stresses going to the places of greatest need. James Gilmour wrote, "Even on the low ground of common sense I seemed to be called to be a missionary. Is the kingdom a harvest field? Then I thought it reasonable that I should seek to work where the work was most abundant and the workers fewest. . . . In place of seeking to assign a reason for going abroad, I would prefer to say that I have failed to discover any reason why I should stay at home."[11] Gordon Olson believes, "If we have a choice and unless there are compelling reasons to the contrary, the Christian worker should choose the place of greatest need! Failure to give adequate consideration to this factor has caused the incredible inequity in the distribution of workers."[12] The benefactor and leader of the Moravian Brethren,

Count Nicholas von Zinzendorf, stated, "I have but one passion—it is He, it is He alone. The world is the field and the field is the world; and henceforth that country shall be my home where I can be most used in winning souls for Christ."[13] This understanding of the missionary call stresses that missionaries receive their calling from God, but then choose the place of their service based on their understanding of greatest need.

Others believe that, while there is a general call to missions, the Holy Spirit must call us to the exact locations where we should serve. Thomas Hale wrote, "This distinction between God's 'general call' and his 'specific call' is very similar to the distinction between God's 'general will' as revealed in Scripture and his 'specific will' for the individual. God's general will (call) is that I be a witness. His specific will (call) is that I be a witness in Nepal, or Chicago, or wherever."[14] Some of the names thus far may be familiar to you, while others are not. Let us consider the lives of some of the best-known missionary heroes and their views of the missionary call.

DAVID BRAINERD (1718–1747)[15]

David Brainerd was a missionary to the indigenous people in the American colonies. He began his missionary career among Native Americans in 1743 and served until his death four years later. Converted at twenty-one, he began missionary service at twenty-five, and died of tuberculosis in the home of his friend Jonathan Edwards, at the tender age of twenty-nine. Edwards published Brainerd's journal, which God has used to challenge and call thousands of missionaries, including William Carey, the father of modern missions.

Brainerd initially felt called to preach and began ministry preparation at Yale. Unfortunately, a casual remark he made offhand in private was reported to the school administration, which resulted in his expulsion. Godly preachers and leaders in New England, who held Brainerd in high regard, sought his reinstatement to the college without success. The doors to the ministry seemed closed to him. However, the Commissioners of the Society in Scotland for Propagating Christian Knowledge examined Brainerd and agreed to send him as "missionary" to the indigenous peoples.

The early stage of his missionary ministry was essentially an intercultural preaching ministry. Brainerd did not initially discern a call to missions, but the missionary call slowly grew to become the passion of his life. After only a couple of years working among the Native Americans, in very harsh conditions, he was offered a pastorate near his hometown. Brainerd turned down the pastorate and other subsequent offers, writing to Jonathan Edwards that he had come to understand his work among the Native Americans to be his calling and purpose for that time in his life. His journal reveals, "Thursday, April 5—Was again much exercised with weakness, and with pain in my head. . . . Resolved to go on still with the Indian affair, if divine providence permitted; although I had before felt some inclination to go to East Hampton, where I was solicited to go."[16]

Brainerd's ministry began with a call to preach, but it developed into a missionary call. Brainerd showed flexibility and responsiveness in his obedience to God's call. When he felt called to preach, he understood that this implied a call to prepare himself and be educated. When the door closed to a preaching ministry, he sought to fulfill his calling in another way. In so doing, he found a missionary call, and in it, the love of his life. The influence of his life and diaries continues to this day. The depth and insight of the spiritual entries in his diary profoundly influence, convict, and encourage thousands of readers who marvel that a young missionary in his twenties wrote them.

We can learn many lessons from David Brainerd. First, God's call is fluid, dynamic, and developing all throughout your life. Second, you must walk by faith and not by sight, always seeking the open window when He closes a door. Third, do not let the disappointments in your life plan make you bitter; use them to make yourself better. Understand that while the plan He has for your life may be radically different from the one you imagined, or thought you would prefer, His plan is a path to peace and fruitful service. Fourth, while He may direct you in ways you did not anticipate, learn to trust the Lord and His loving plan for you.

WILLIAM CAREY (1761–1834)[17]

William Carey was called to pastor a small Baptist congregation not long after beginning work as a schoolmaster. Carey was a gifted natural linguist and had a thirst to know about the peoples of the world. He taught himself languages, learning six by the age of twenty-one, and read as much as he could about the nations and cultures of the world. Reading Captain Cook's journals, he wrote the languages, people names, and all other data he could find on scraps of leather that he fashioned into a world map. As he read The Last Voyage of Captain Cook and the Life and Diary of David Brainerd, he developed a passion for reaching the lost "heathen" with the gospel of Jesus Christ. George Smith recounted,

> In the school-hours as he tried to teach the children geography and the Bible and was all the while teaching himself, the missionary idea arose in his mind, and his soul became fired with the self-consecration, unknown to Wiclif and Huss, Luther and Calvin, Knox and even Bunyan, for theirs was other work. All his past knowledge of nature and of books, all his favourite reading of voyages and of travels which had led his schoolfellows to dub him Columbus, all his painful study of the Word, his experiences of the love of Christ and expoundings of the meaning of His message to men for six years, were gathered up, were intensified, and were directed with a concentrated power to the thought that Christ died, as for him, so for these millions of dark savages whom Cook was revealing to Christendom, and who had never heard the glad tidings of great joy.[18]

The desperate plight and need of the nations who had never heard the gospel profoundly moved Carey. He was particularly burdened by the spiritual need reflected in the stories. God used his global awareness to convince him of the need for a missions movement to reach the heathen. He began to grow in his understanding that if it is the duty of all men to believe the gospel, then it is the church's duty to make it known among all nations. He responded, "Here am I; send me!" Carey felt that the call was from God. Mary Drewery describes Carey's understanding of this divine call. "There is no doubt that Carey did feel called by God. He continues the letter to his father . . . with the words: 'I am not my own, nor would I choose for myself. Let God employ me where he thinks fit, and give me patience and discretion to fill up my station to his honour and glory.'"[19]

Carey persevered through significant hindrances as he attempted to fulfill his missionary call. The other ministers in his association did not initially share his concern for the nations, ships headed to India from England would not carry anyone without a license to go, and no licenses were granted to those who intended to engage in missionary work. Additionally, as previously noted, Carey keenly felt the missionary call, but his wife did not. This must have made the difficult decision to leave behind home and kin unbelievably stressful.

Carey's sense of his missionary call grew out of an awareness of the biblical commands to evangelize the lost and minister to the spiritual needs of the peoples of the world. He clearly viewed the call of God as superior to every other obligation in his life—wife, children, home, and country. Like Carey, our sense of profound calling should drive us to overcome initial hindrances and pioneer in strategies and methodologies that will result in fruit that abides. Carey worked hard, suffered greatly, and learned patience through barren years. Yet, his perseverance resulted in a legacy that continues to this day in India.

JOHN G. PATON (1824–1907)[20]

John Paton was born in Scotland in 1824. His devout father made a covenant with God to give his children to the Lord for ministry. This godly heritage was not lost on Paton and he was ministry-minded from an early age. While still a youth, he discerned a call to missions and moved forty miles away to train in theological and medical studies while working as a city missionary in Glasgow.

Paton also struggled with hindrances to fulfilling his missionary call. Medical problems he experienced when he arrived in Glasgow for training required him to return home for a period to regain his health. Then, changes at the school closed the door to his education for a time. He eventually returned to his training and spent a total of nine years ministering in Glasgow. Yet, he felt that God wanted something else for him. Theodore Mueller observed,

> John Paton was very happy in his City Mission work, and convinced that the Lord's abundant blessings rested upon it. Yet though both he and his pious parents rejoiced in this, he was always troubled "with the wail of the perishing heathen in the South Seas." Steadily he had pursued his theological studies, until he had completed the prescribed course and could be ordained as a minister of his church. But he felt that all the work he had done so far was but preparatory to his real calling; his earnest desire was to serve God in the foreign mission field.[21]

When he spoke of foreign missionary service, there were objections from family and friends. "Every attempt was made to induce him to reverse his decision. He was offered 'any reasonable salary' with a fine manse if he would only stay, whereas the Mission Directors could only allow him six hundred dollars a year if he went to the New Hebrides. When it was found that money would not hold him in Glasgow, his friends tried to fill him with fear. 'Remember the cannibals!' they said; 'you will be eaten by cannibals!' "[22]

However, Paton's peace shines through in his response, "If I die here in Glasgow, I shall be eaten by worms; if I can but live and die serving the Lord Jesus, it will make no difference to me whether I am eaten by cannibals or by worms; for in the Great Day my resurrection body will arise as fair as yours in the likeness of our risen Redeemer."[23] Taking a wife, he was married only two weeks before departing for the field.

We can see his understanding of the missionary call in his writings. His missionary call made him willing to go anywhere, regardless of the potential cost. Paton knew that the call demanded sacrifice. He sacrificed much, burying his young wife and children on the field, but stayed true to his calling.

J. HUDSON TAYLOR (1832–1905)[24]

Hudson Taylor was born to faithful Christian parents and when he experienced a radical conversion as a teenager, he prayed that God would use him in missions. Initially, he resisted a commitment to medical school, fearing that it could prevent his departure for the field when the door opened, but then realized the value such training would have in China for mission work. Intrigued by the thought of going to China as a missionary, he pursued that path and studied books about life and ministry in China. "Hudson early made up his mind to go to China as a missionary, and his interest in the land was increased by a little book called 'China' which he read and reread until he almost knew it by heart."[25] Taylor prepared himself physically by eating a simple diet and giving up many physical comforts. He strongly believed in dependence upon God for financial means and support of his ministry. His pious parents had prayed him to the field. In fact, his father had actually prayed that he would become a missionary in China, although he did not learn of this until after he had arrived in China.

Taylor's early ministry became a model for other missions efforts as he sought to master the language and contextualize his ministry into the culture. He eventually established the China Inland Mission with the intention of reaching into the unreached interior of the country. His understanding of the missionary call is one aspect of his legacy. Daniel Bacon wrote, "He never reduced God's call to a pet formula, nor did he persuade on the basis of need alone. The commands of Scripture, the needs of the world, and the general circumstances of the believer were all significant factors to be prayerfully considered."[26] Taylor himself wrote of his call, "Never shall I forget . . . the feeling that came over me then. Words can never describe it. I felt I was in the presence of God, entering into the covenant with the Almighty. I felt as though I wished to withdraw my promise, but could not. Something seemed to say, 'Your prayer is answered, your conditions are accepted.' And from that time the conviction never left me that I was called to China."[27]

In fact, the call to location was a central focus of Hudson Taylor's understanding of the missionary call. Perhaps this was because he sought to mobilize people who were specifically called to China—for China Inland Mission. Taylor said, "It will not do to say that you have no special call to go to China. With these facts before you, you need rather to ascertain whether you have a special call to stay at home. If in the sight of God you cannot say you are sure that you have a special call to stay at home, why are you disobeying the Saviour's plain command to go?"[28] Taylor is well known for the perspective that every Christian has some kind of missionary call by his oft-quoted phrase, "The Great Commission is not an option to be considered; it is a command to be obeyed."[29] J. Hudson Taylor understood the missionary call to be motivated by the neediest places, geographic specificity, and the belief that the God who calls would meet all needs.

CHARLOTTE "LOTTIE" DIGGES MOON (1840–1912)[30]

Lottie Moon was one of Southern Baptist's earliest missionaries, serving in China for nearly forty years. Her name is easily recognized as it rings out in SBC churches every Christmas season; the annual international missions offering is named in her honor, remembering her death on Christmas Eve on board a ship bound for America. She had given of her personal means to feed starving Chinese in a time of famine to the degree that her body was weakened beyond recovery.

Lottie Moon struggled with a call to international missions for a time, but found Southern Baptists reluctant to appoint and send a single female. Even so, she surrendered to God's call in February of 1873 upon hearing a sermon on John 4:35, "Do you not say, 'There are yet four months, then comes the harvest'? Look, I tell you, lift up your eyes, and see that the fields are white for harvest." The Foreign Mission Board of the Southern Baptist Convention was changing in its views at that time and appointed Lottie Moon as their first female missionary to China in July of the same year. Wyatt Rogers writes, "After several years of persistent effort, she won an appointment as a single woman missionary. Her deep commitment and a strong call to Christian work, together with dogged determination, were the keys to her appointment and her long and successful career."[31] Lottie Moon heard the call from Jesus' words recorded in the biblical text. Lottie was tireless in her correspondence back to Mission headquarters in Virginia, pleading for more who were called to missions. Toward the end of her career, she wrote, "I pray that no missionary will ever be as lonely as I have been."[32]

AMY CARMICHAEL (1867–1951)[33]

Amy Carmichael felt God's missionary call on her life after hearing the great missions mobilizer, J. Hudson Taylor, speaking at a Keswick conference in 1887. In a letter to her mother after surrendering to God's missionary call, she wrote, "I went to my own room and just asked the Lord what it all meant, what did He wish me to do, and, Mother, as clearly as I ever heard you speak, I heard Him say, 'GO YE.' I never heard it just so plainly before; I cannot be mistaken for I know He spoke. He says 'Go,' I cannot stay."[34] After a little more than a year serving in Japan, she began her life-long ministry in India. Like Taylor, she sought to contextualize her ministry to the culture and clothing of the people among whom she worked. Specifically, her ministry was rescuing young girls from a life of temple prostitution.

A bad fall left Amy bedridden for the last twenty years of her life, but she remained in India, and began to reflect and write about the Christian life and being a missionary. She wrote, "Missionary life is simply a chance to die."[35] Her call to missionary service was not as bound to location as Hudson Taylor's. Her initial understanding of where to serve was Japan, but she was redirected after fifteen months. However, her general sense of the missionary call never wavered. Amy knew she was to go as a missionary, discovered where God was leading, and once she got there and got to know the people, lived her life discovering all the ways she was to serve. She provided shelter, cared for children, and rescued the helpless. Although faced with great odds, she felt God's missionary call and was faithful to it. Lois Dick writes, "Amy, frail in health, subject to neuralgia and headaches, the financial supporter of her widowed mother who was left with seven children, the least likely to pioneer in a pagan land, was called by God. An old, oft repeated story. God uses nobodies, foolish things, things that are nothing. For so she considered herself."[36]

CAM TOWNSEND (1896–1982)[37]

Cam Townsend grew up in a godly home where he heard his father close his prayers at every meal with the promise recorded in Numbers 14:21, Isaiah 11:9, and Habakkuk 2:14: "May the earth be filled with the knowledge of the glory of the LORD as the waters cover the sea." No doubt this reverberated in his consciousness all of his life. In 1917, Cam and a friend went to Guatemala to sell Bibles. Townsend's Bible sales did not fare well because most of the peoples he met could not read Spanish. Additionally, many were monolingual in indigenous languages. Townsend was burdened to bring the Word of God to the peoples of the world in their mother tongue.

Cam Townsend experienced a growing and developing call to missions. He probably did not intend his Bible-selling days to be a lifelong career. James and Marti Hefley describe the uncertainty: "During his sophomore year Cam was drawn to the Student Volunteer Band, the local arm of the national Student Volunteer Movement. New joiners had to tell why they wanted to be members . . . when his turn came, he found it hard to articulate his concern for foreign missions. He could only say, 'I'm not sure why I wish to belong.'"[38] Yet, God honored his obedience to the growing call.

His interest picked up, however, when John R. Mott, the leader of the movement, came to the campus to speak. Cam sensed the burden of the man and wondered if there might not be a place for him overseas. He was further challenged by the life of Hudson Taylor, founder of the fifty-year-old China Inland Mission. Taylor's faith, pioneering, and adaptation to the Chinese culture appealed to him. He felt that if God should lead him to become a missionary, he would strive to be like this man. [39]

In the path of continued obedience, God swept a missionary call into his life. The fruit of this call is Bibles and Bible translation projects underway in the heart language of hundreds of ethnolinguistic people groups around the world. Townsend's sense of call was driven by the need to share God's Word in culturally and linguistically appropriate ways. He established Camp Wycliffe to train linguists to join him in this vision. He later founded the Summer Institute of Linguistics and Wycliffe Bible Translators.

Townsend's heartbeat resonated with William Carey's; he keenly felt the need of the peoples of the world's language groups to have God's Word in their own language. Being a man of vision and passion, when his supervisors closed the door to this ministry, he found a window, and called it Wycliffe Bible Translators.

JIM ELLIOT (1927–1956)[40]

Jim Elliot is one of the most influential missionaries of modern times. Although God used him powerfully in other ways, his most compelling missions sermon was preached in the way he left this world, which continues to challenge men and women everywhere. I recently shared the pulpit at a missions conference with a couple who were retiring after fifty years of service in South America. I shook my head in silent awe as I heard words echoing through the room that I have heard from many, many others: "When I heard the news of the martyrdom of Jim Elliot and the other missionaries in the jungles of Ecuador, I said, 'Here am I, Lord; Send me.'" Indeed, names like Jim Elliot, Nate Saint, Pete Fleming, Roger Youderian, Ed McCully, Ecuador, Aucas, and Palm Beach bring to mind the perfect picture of obedience unto death. Although this story is repeated in similar fashion throughout the pages of missions history, this one happened in recent times, on our side of the world, and in a jungle that continues very much as it did in January 1956.

Jim Elliot was a profoundly serious and committed Christian man. Like Carey, the numbers and needs of the lands where Christ had not been preached motivated him. Jim challenged others to consider missions and not spend their lives where others were already doing the work. After his death, Jim's wife, Elisabeth, edited and published his journal where we see the obvious influence of the world's needs on his missionary call.

> This notebook was found on the Curaray beach after Jim's death, its pages scattered along the sand, some washed clean of ink, others stained with mud and rain but still legible. Besides the names of hundreds of people for whom Jim prayed [there are] several pages of mission statistics written while in college, of which the following is an excerpt:
>
> "1700 languages have not a word of the Bible translated. 90% of the people who volunteer for the mission field never

get there. It takes more than a 'Lord, I'm willing!' 64% of the world have never heard of Christ. 5000 people die every hour. The population of India equals that of North America, Africa, and South America combined. There is one missionary for every 71,000 people there. There is one Christian worker for every 50,000 people in foreign lands, while there is one to every 500 in the United States."

In view of the unequivocal command of Christ, coupled with these staggering facts, Jim believed that if he stayed in the United States the burden of proof would lie with him to show that he was justified in so doing.[41]

As a very committed believer, Jim was challenged both by statistics about the needs of the world and the numbers not going. His time at Wheaton College continued to confirm a growing *sense of ought* to go. His relationships and interaction with other students such as Dave Howard, Pete Fleming, and Elisabeth Howard, among others, reinforced his sense of call. Exploring his understanding of the call resulted in knowing not only where God was calling him, but also the people group and the specific location.

Elisabeth wrote that when he left their home in Shandia to join the others in Operation Auca, he walked out the screen door and did not look back. She writes of his response to her when she asked whether he was sure he was supposed to go to the Aucas: "'I am called,' was the simple reply. So, it was all right. Scriptural principles, God-directed circumstances, and own inward assurance were consonant."[42] One of the keys of his influence was that he felt his missionary call so clearly that he could calmly walk to his own death for Christ's sake. For Jim Elliot and many martyrs more, the call to obedience was a call to die. That was part of God's plan for their lives, and the glory of God is in that, too.

CONCLUSION

THE MISSIONARY HEROES and well-known Christian leaders of the past have held differing opinions about the missionary call and each received their call in a unique way. Some notable missionary calls flowed from the *sense of ought* that all Christians should feel, others from a knowledge of the spiritual darkness of a lost world, an audible voice, a global awareness that grew and became increasingly focused, and simple obedience to the revealed will of God in His Word. None of these is wrong, but none is normative and prescriptive either. That means that you should not determine the legitimacy of your call by comparing it to someone else's experience. God calls every Christian in the way that He knows is best. He made our ears and knows the call we will hear the best. He also made our hearts and filled them with desires that He longs to fulfill. As helpful as it is to see how He called men and women through the years, it is more important to embrace His call to you when it comes.

12

UNDERSTANDING AND ANSWERING THE MISSIONARY CALL

WHAT IS THE MISSIONARY CALL? Thousands of sincere Christian missionaries each describe their calls in many different ways. Yet, God's Word, missiologists, and the testimony of our missionary heroes echo in agreement about common components of the ways that God leads Christians to be involved in missions. This call includes an awareness of the needs of, and a concern for, a lost world; obedience to the commands of Christ; a radical commitment to God; your church's recognition of your gifts; a fervent desire and passion for missions; and the Spirit's gifting. The missionary call is God's method for moving His children to intercultural service and sustaining them in the work He designed for them before the creation of the world (Acts 17:26).

Many have wondered exactly how specific the missionary call must be. Some new missions students have sheepishly confessed to me that they were not yet sure where God was calling them, as if the absence of a zip code brings their missionary call into doubt. The missionary call is not as much about the exact neighborhood where you are to serve as it is a sustained burden to see hell-bound souls around the world redeemed by the blood of the Lamb. It is a yearning to see all the nations fall before the throne to worship Christ, and a radical surrender of all one has and is for His glory. It is a fervent desire to cross any and every barrier to share the saving gospel of God's grace: language barriers, geographic barriers, socioeconomic barriers, and cultural barriers. This is what we think of as the inward call. It is essential to understand that the beginning of a missionary call rarely includes all the details of timing, mission agency, location, language, or people group. The external call refers to the recognition of your gifting for missionary service—both by your own reckoning as well as by affirmation from your local church fellowship. It includes the fit with a mission agency and team, the confirmation that comes through raising support, and the fruit that grows out of a missions-saturated life.

The missionary calling is pervasive, irrevocable, and ever increasing as it touches every area of your life. Christians fulfill their missionary call in many ways. John R. Mott wanted to go to the mission field, but he remained in the United States and fulfilled his calling by traveling, preaching, and mobilizing others to international missions. William Carey went to India, served with great distinction through his lifelong career there, and ultimately went from his home in India to his home in heaven. Jim Elliot fulfilled his calling by going to the jungles of Ecuador for only a few years until he was martyred by the Huaorani people he was trying to evangelize. My former college professor fulfilled his missionary calling by going to serve in Korea for five years before returning to a Christian college in the United States where he taught and encouraged hundreds of young students to consider missions. Ralph Winter fulfilled his missionary calling by serving in Guatemala, and then returning home to the United States to establish and preside over the U.S. Center for World Mission from where he has mobilized and equipped thousands to go into the world. I know a missionary whose missionary call is to work among Iranians. Interestingly, he lives and works among these people in Atlanta, Georgia. Some are surprised to learn that his missionary call finds its expression in working with these people in the United States, but in our age of globalization, intercultural missionaries may serve faithfully and never leave their home country. The missionary call is for life and all its legitimate expressions would fill another book. Additionally, the ways and places you fulfill your missionary call may vary through the entirety of your life. It is important to recognize and distinguish between the missionary call and God's guidance in how you fulfill it.

At the beginning of our pilgrimage together, we noticed that there are three basic understandings of the missionary call that have enjoyed particular prominence in missions history. One understanding denies the existence of a missionary call, since the New Testament does not mention the call, gift, or office of missionary. Therefore, they would say that a Christian might choose to be a missionary in the same way one chooses to be a plumber, doctor, or farmer. The second understanding is that there is indeed a missionary call and we all have one; it is the Great Commission. Thus, all Christians should go to the nations and make disciples, and the burden of proof is upon every believer who does not go to give credible evidence that God has called him to stay at home. The third understanding is that because the life of a missionary is very dangerous and is a special position in gospel ministry, no one should attempt to go without a clear and personal missionary call. This position holds, "If you are not called, you had better not try to go, and if you are, you had better not try to stay."

Each of these positions is partially right—and wrong when taken to an extreme. First, while the Bible does not mention the missionary call, it certainly describes God's heart for the nations and His desire for us to join Him on mission. Second, yes, Jesus commissioned all believers to make disciples and imitate Him, but He called Paul and Barnabas in a unique way to advance His kingdom where the gospel had not been preached. The church in

Jerusalem was not seeking to fulfill the Great Commission until after the martyrdom of Stephen, when the believers scattered and regrouped in Antioch. It was there that they began to evangelize Greeks in addition to the Jews. When the Spirit set Paul and Barnabas apart, He did not rebuke the larger church for not going, nor did He call all to go. They were to be missions-minded, but not necessarily missionaries. Nowhere in Paul's writings does he exhort all believers to go—even on short-term missions as he did. Clearly, there is a distinction between those who are to go and those who are to send. Third, while I argue that there definitely is a missionary call, we must be responsible in our use of the term; each missionary describes the call in a different way. It is counterproductive to exhort people not to go unless they are sure they have been called, unless you also explain to them what you mean by "called."

The missionary call also includes the profound sense of a God-stirred ought, a burden for lost souls in a dying world, a burning desire to see every people group in the world prostrate in worship before the throne of God. It is a recognition of the gifts and abilities that God has given you mixed with the desire to go where your life can best be spent "to take hold of that for which Christ Jesus took hold of [you]" (Philippians 3:12 NIV). It is at once subtle and overpowering, sudden and growing, understood and yet becoming clearer all your life.

Yes, there is a personal missionary call, and it is so personal that no one else can truly comprehend it fully. In the absence of clear teaching on the missionary call, many mistakenly assume that it must come in a vision, an audible voice, undeniable circumstances, or some other supernatural revelation. In fact, the unexplained term, "the missionary call," is one of the most common reasons that some do not go into missions. Many give testimonies such as, "I love sharing the gospel and being around internationals. I am fascinated with languages and I really enjoy learning as much as I can about different cultures. I love to travel and wish I could live overseas to serve God in missions. I just wish He would call me." Then, they sit at home waiting for a vision in the night, writing in the sky, or a deep, booming voice from heaven calling their name.

You cannot determine your missionary call simply by comparing it against an objective list of required components. The Bible does not describe such a call, nor does it set forth the essentials for a missionary call. An old sermon illustration speaks of all the blind men that Jesus healed. One day the healed men are sitting around and talking about how Jesus restored their sight. The story goes that one man says, "Oh, do you remember how wonderful it was when He made the mud and put it on your eyes and told you to go wash?" Then another healed man says, "He never put mud on my eyes, He just touched me." Then, after an animated discussion, the first man declares the second still to be blind, saying that he could not possibly be able to see without experiencing the mud in the healing process! We create the same confusion when we compare missionary calls. Jesus calls each of us in diverse circumstances and in unique ways.

We pray for the nations asking that God would pour out His Spirit and send awakening to the lost peoples of the world. Jesus commanded us also to pray to the Lord of the harvest asking that He send out workers into the harvest field (Matthew 9:38). The missionary call is how He does this. When friends, children, parents, or church staff members announce that God has stirred their hearts for the nations and called them to some mission field, the God-honoring response is not rending of garments, but celebration. Just as we praise Him when He miraculously answers prayers to heal, save, or deliver, we should praise Him when He answers our prayers to send out workers—even when He calls them from our own homes.

The anxiety over following God's leading into missions and exploring a missionary call is understandable. The wave of terrorism that covers the globe certainly gives just reason to pause. Working through the issues of the missionary call and knowing

God's will is wise. However, when anxiety swells, do not let fear make the decision for you. Remember that the world has known terrorism in varying degrees since the fall of man. Throughout the years, wars, religious persecution, kidnappings, piracy on the high seas, unprovoked attacks from "savage Indians," and exotic diseases have been harsh realities in missionaries' lives. The dangers that exist are real, but only illustrate the fact that men and women need Christ. The suffering and dying of missionaries have advanced the Kingdom as nothing else could and the blood of the saints has ever been the seed and fuel of gospel advance. When your fears obscure a clear vision of your missionary call, consider whether the fear is from possible suffering and persecution or from an honest assessment of your gifts and abilities. Fear can be healthy and appropriate in proper perspective, but do not let it overwhelm you, govern your life, and hinder your obedience to God's missionary call.

Hearing God's missionary call has a great deal to do with what you are listening *for*. Herbert Kane's advice was that you should not sit around with your arms folded waiting for a lightning bolt or a vision from God to call you to missions. He counseled those who were listening for God's missionary call to maintain an open mind, an attentive ear, a pure heart, busy hands, and ready feet.[1] However, he also stressed that even after you do all of that, the call is still subjective, reminding us that even the apostle Paul said in I Corinthians 7:40, "I think that I too have the Spirit of God." The story is told of a Native American walking with a friend during the noise and madness of Manhattan at midday. In the midst of horns blaring, taxis screeching, and subways rushing, he said, "I hear a cricket." His friend said it was impossible, but he walked over to a planter and found it under a bush. The Native American told him that you hear what you are listening for. To make his point, he dropped a handful of change on the sidewalk and every head within twenty feet turned to look.[2] What are you listening for?

When you know that God is leading you to embrace a missionary call, many questions about where, with whom, when, and how begin to crowd your mind. First, follow the steps to be assured of God's will, and then seek counsel from the agencies that you are considering. Prepare yourself and take definite steps to go; do not rest in good intentions and daydreams. Answering the missionary call will bring many changes into your life, and that awareness is frightening. Courage is an essential trait for every step of the missionary life: willingness to listen for the call, answering the call, seeking appointment and raising support—even more so for when you say good-bye and leave everything familiar, learning a new language and culture, and living and raising children in another country. However, never forget that to enjoy the blessings, grace, peace, mercy, challenges, rewards, and the high privilege of a missionary call, these steps are necessary—and God-ordered, too.

We come now to the end of our pilgrimage together to understand the missionary call and find your place in God's world. Let me encourage you to be faithful to His calling when you clearly hear it. I commend you for your willingness to listen for and explore the call, and for willingness to make the sacrifice. Remember that God is in control; He has a plan to reach the ones needing to hear and He has a people He is preparing and calling to go. Stay focused through the process. A thousand voices will present passionate arguments about why you should not go. The sacrifice will appear too great. If you do not stay focused, you will slip into the American dream pattern of borrowing to live at a standard that Madison Avenue assures you is what you deserve and need, or you may marry someone who does not wish or qualify to go to the mission field.

Yes, there is a personal missionary call, and it is so personal that no one else can comprehend it fully. My prayer is that, if God is calling you to missions, you will hear and respond to His call, and if He is not, that you will stay and follow His leading. In chapter 2, we considered the children's catechism question, "How can you glorify God?" and its answer, "By loving Him and doing what He commands." We have also considered Psalm 37:4, "Delight yourself in the LORD, and he will give you the desires of your heart." What are the desires of your heart?

ACKNOWLEDGMENTS

NO ONE HAS EVER WRITTEN a book without the help that God provided through hundreds of people. Where does one begin in thanking those who have had a part in the formation of skills, thinking, worldview, and all the encouragement? Does one begin with Sunday school or kindergarten teachers of the formative years? What about all the friends without whom you would not be the person you are, much less think the way you think? It is impossible to name everyone, and so the temptation is to forgo any thanks for fear of omitting key helpers. Still, I must mention some who contributed significantly to make this book a reality.

When God saved me, the "Moody" name became significant in my spiritual development; I took a couple of Moody correspondence courses as first steps in my new life. Now, with this book, the people at Moody are a blessing once again. Many thanks to the great people at Moody Publishers; editors Paul Santhouse, Lisa Major, Jennifer Lyell, and Chris Reese have been a great encouragement to me in this process; marketing brand manager

Holly Kisly has also shown tremendous energy for this project. I am grateful to each of you.

I am also thankful to all my colleagues and friends at The Southern Baptist Theological Seminary. Thanks to Drs. Al Mohler and Thom Rainer for giving me the privilege of joining the faculty here. Dr. Mohler has amassed an excellent faculty that attracts fantastic students and the resulting environment is both warmly evangelical and profoundly academic, and aims to glorify Jesus Christ. Thanks also to my dean, Chuck Lawless, for his Christian testimony, burden for the nations, and great example of a writing academician who remains very involved in local church ministry. Thanks to all of my colleagues in the Billy Graham School of Missions, Evangelism and Church Growth: George, Tim, Jim, J. D., Vaughn, Ted, Bryan, Hayward, Adam, Bill, and Paul. Thank you for your warm friendship and encouragement.

To my students at SBTS and around the world go my deepest thanks for encouraging, teaching, challenging, and sharpening me, and for enduring hours of lectures on these topics as they took shape in my heart and mind. I have learned more from you than you ever have or shall from me. You have made this book possible.

To my pastor and friend, Dr. Bill Cook, the staff, and all my fellow church members at the Ninth and O Baptist Church—and especially the prayer warriors in my Sunday school class—thank you for allowing me to serve you in missions leadership. Thanks for going with me repeatedly to Ecuador and Peru and for letting me watch as God called some of you with your own missionary calling.

To Mary, my best and ever-constant friend, thank you for encouraging me when I felt this project was too far beyond me. I am so thankful to know that, through it all, you have always been and will always be by me. You are a great blessing to me and I thank God for you.

To Christopher and Molly, you are more than just my two great children; you are my precious friends. We talk about everything, cheer each other on, and laugh—A LOT. The joy and laughter you bring into our home is one of God's richest blessings to me. I am so proud of you for who you are and what you do. When I think of your mom and the two of you, I say with David, "Truly the boundary lines have fallen for me in pleasant places." I am very thankful to you and mom for allowing me the time necessary to write this book.

I am also thankful to all the real-life missionary heroes I have known who have shown me what it is to hear and remain faithful to God's missionary call through the good times and the hard times.

Finally, thank You, Lord, for the grace, pardon, mercy, peace, and joy that You shower into my life daily. I am humbled that You would call and use me to advance Your kingdom and glorify Your Name in the world—and now this book! I am humbled like David, "Then King David went in and sat before the LORD and said, 'Who am I, O Lord God, and what is my house, that you have brought me thus far?'" (2 Samuel 7:18).

GLOSSARY

OVERALL

Missionary—In the context of this book, an individual who crosses cultural and/or linguistic barriers for the purpose of making disciples.

Missionary Call—The missionary call includes an awareness of the needs of a lost world, the commands of Christ, a concern for the lost, a radical commitment to God, your church's blessing and commissioning, a fervent desire, the Spirit's gifting, your passion, and an indescribable yearning that motivates beyond all understanding.

INTRODUCTION

Globalization—The effect of greater awareness, interconnectedness, and spread of common issues and trends across countries around the world.

Urbanization—The worldwide trend of movement from rural areas to urban areas.

Pluralism—The belief that all religions share equal value and provide a means of salvation.

Creative-access Platforms—An occupation or explanation sufficient to qualify for residency in a country that does not admit missionaries.

Ethnocentrism—The tendency of everyone to judge all cultures by their own home culture. In the process, the new culture virtually always is seen as inferior, inefficient, wrong, and lacking.

CHAPTER ONE

Ethnolinguistic Group (also referred to as "people group")—Refers to the identification of people based upon their common culture, language, values, and self-identification rather than geopolitical boundaries or mere racial identification. Missiologically, an ethnolinguistic group is the largest group across which the gospel can spread without crossing cultural or language barriers.

CHAPTER THREE

Protoevangelion—"The first gospel" as found in Genesis 3:15, with God's promise to redeem man through the seed of the woman and the crushing of the serpent.

The Great Commission—The command of Jesus to go to the ethnolinguistic groups of the world and make disciples (Matthew 28:18–20; Mark 16:15–16; Luke 24:47; John 20:21; Acts 1:8).

The Great Commandments—The two greatest commandments as given by Christ to first love the Lord your God with all your heart, soul, and mind, and second to love your neighbor as yourself (Matthew 22:34–40).

The Great Compassion—Reflected in the compassion and love of Christ to reach and teach the multitudes and also personified in us when we consider the needs of the world and the lostness of people.

CHAPTER FOUR

Hyper-Calvinism—The unbiblical doctrine that overemphasizes the sovereignty of God and deemphasizes the responsibility of man, leaving man without any true responsibility to seek the fulfillment of the commands of Christ.

Creative-access Platform Missionaries—Missionaries who have gained residency in a country that does not legally allow Christian missionaries by stating an educational or occupational purpose other than ministry.

Tentmaker Missionaries—Missionaries who work with the purpose of reaching the people and participating in missions efforts, but support themselves through full-time secular employment rather than full-time traditional missionary support.

Indigenous—Anything that is native to a land or country.

Faith Missions—Missions efforts funded solely through donations by individuals or local churches.

Missiologist—An individual who studies the theology, philosophy, and methodology of missions for the purpose of advancing the kingdom through missionaries.

Culture—The common beliefs, behaviors, values, norms, and "rules of the game for life" held by a group of individuals.

Worldview—The lens through which an individual views the world, answers ultimate questions of reality, and processes information and experiences.

Syncretism—The process of blending together two belief systems in a way that results in a third. Evangelical missionaries use the term to refer to the confusion of religions when former religions are mixed with the gospel, resulting in a religion contrary to the teachings of Christianity.

Contextualization—Adapting the forms of Christianity to the cultural settings of the world in ways that are faithful to God's Word, but are culturally appropriate for the target people.

People Group (also referred to as "ethnolinguistic group")—
Refers to the identification of people based upon their
common culture, language, values, and self-identification
rather than geopolitical boundaries or mere racial identification. Missiologically, a people group is the largest group
across which the gospel can spread without crossing cultural
or language barriers.

Unreached People Group—A people group among which there is
no indigenous community of believing Christians with adequate numbers and resources to evangelize this people group.
The original Joshua Project editorial committee selected the
criterion of less than 2 percent evangelical Christian.[1]

Search Theology—Advocates identifying the unreached pockets
of the world and proclaiming the gospel there.

Harvest Theology—Advocates focusing missions efforts on the
peoples and places where God is already working.

CHAPTER FIVE

Furlough (also referred to as "stateside assignment")—Refers to
the period of time when missionaries return to their home
country for several months or a year prior to returning to the
mission field.

Majority World—Increasingly used to refer to the Third World or
Two-Thirds World.

CHAPTER SIX

Short-term Missions—Historically, any missions work that is less
than lifetime service, but increasingly refers to terms of service
of a few weeks to a few years.

Career Missions—Full-time vocational engagement in missions
for the duration of a lifelong career.

Animistic—Cultures that hold to the belief system that the world is governed by invisible forces and spirits that must be pacified or manipulated through rites and rituals in order to avoid misfortune, increase blessings, or counter sorcery.

Shamans—In animistic cultures, an individual who acts as a mediator between the visible and unseen forces of the world through the practice of rites, rituals, and offerings.

CHAPTER SEVEN

Paternalism—The practice of missionaries perpetually providing for or managing the national church and national church leaders rather than training them to grow toward self-sufficiency.

CHAPTER EIGHT

Full-salary Model—The model some missions agencies and parachurch organizations use by paying their missionaries a salary rather than requiring that the missionary raise any portion of the financial support through donations.

Support-raising Model—The model used by the majority of missions agencies that requires missionaries to fund at least a portion of their work and/or salary through self-solicited donations from individuals and local churches.

Creative-access Countries—Countries that do not allow individuals to obtain a visa or residency for the purpose of Christian missionary efforts or Christian ministry. It is into these countries that missionaries often use a creative-access platform to gain entry.

Calvinists—Commonly used to refer to individuals who hold to the doctrines of total depravity, unconditional election, limited atonement, irresistible grace, and perseverance of the saints, recognizing the overarching significance of God's sovereignty in the work of salvation and sanctification.

Arminians—Commonly used to refer to individuals who deny the teachings of Calvinism, and prefer free will, human responsibility, and the universal nature of the atonement, thus emphasizing man's role in the work of salvation and sanctification.

Polygamy—The practice of having more than one spouse at any given time.

CHAPTER NINE

Culture Shock—The period of adjustment that comes when living in a new culture in which your sense of what is normal is no longer accepted as normal for the host culture.

Country Shock—The stress and tension that accompany a move to a country with significant differences of altitude, temperature, food, rhythm of life, driving patterns, etc.

CHAPTER TEN

Role Deprivation—The grief resulting from the loss of identification and sense of purpose that is associated with one's ministry or occupational role once an individual arrives on the mission field.

Cultural Adaptation—The healthy response to culture shock that is characterized by adjusting to the norms and expectations of the host culture without losing one's sense of self-identification and association with the home culture.

CHAPTER ELEVEN

Keswick—An annual meeting held in England beginning in the 1870s for the purpose of promoting holiness. Although not an emphasis at the beginning, missions increasingly found its way into the movement and many missionaries trace their pilgrimage to these meetings. Eventually, the Keswick conference profoundly influenced the history of missions.

Sense of Ought—The internal conviction that convinces an individual that regardless of the circumstances or perceived hurdles, they must serve the Lord in missions because of the needs of a lost world, God-given abilities for the work, the heart of God, and the commands of Christ.

1. Joshua Project, "Unreached People Groups," http://www.joshuaproject.net/definitions.php.

NOTES

INTRODUCTION

1. J. Herbert Kane, *Understanding Christian Missions* (Grand Rapids, MI: Baker Book House, 1974), 38.

2. Christopher J. H. Wright, *The Mission of God: Unlocking the Bible's Grand Narrative* (Downers Grove, IL: InterVarsity, 2006).

3. Ralph D. Winter and Steven Hawthorne, *Perspectives on the World Christian Movement* (Pasadena, CA: William Carey Library, 1999).

4. See glossary for definitions of common missiological terms used throughout the book.

5. Mark Twain, *The Innocents Abroad* (Leipzig: Bernhard Tauchnitz, 1879), 333.

6. Ralph D. Winter, "Are You Finding Your Way Into God's Highest Call for You?" *Mission Frontiers*, January/February 2007: 5.

CHAPTER ONE: UNDERSTANDING THE MISSIONARY CALL

1. Joshua Project, "Global Statistics," http://www.joshuaproject.net/globalstatistics.php.

2. Phil Bogosian, "The Time Has Not Yet Come: Why America Is Experiencing Judgment," *Mission Frontiers*, March/April (1992), http://www.missionfrontiers.org/1992/0304/ma928.htm.

3. Jennifer Nault, *Georgia* (New York: Weigl, 2002), 14.

4. Thomas Hale, *On Being a Missionary* (Pasadena, CA: William Carey Library, 1995), 18.

CHAPTER TWO: HOW CAN I KNOW GOD'S WILL?

1. Elisabeth Elliot, *A Slow and Certain Light* (Waco, TX: Word Books, 1975), 20.
2. J. I. Packer, *Knowing God* (Downers Grove, IL: InterVarsity, 1993).
3. J. Herbert Kane, *The Making of a Missionary* (Grand Rapids, MI: Baker Book House, 1975), 29.
4. Ibid., 30.
5. Henry T. Blackaby, *Experiencing God* (Nashville, TN: Broadman and Holman, 2004), 176.
6. Oswald Chambers, *My Utmost for His Highest* (Uhrichsville, OH: Discovery House, 1992), Sept 23.

CHAPTER THREE: IS THERE A BIBLICAL BASIS FOR THE MISSIONARY CALL?

1. John Piper, *Let the Nations Be Glad!* (Grand Rapids, MI: Baker Books, 1993), 11.
2. Matthew Henry, *Matthew Henry's Commentary on the Whole Bible: Acts–Revelation* (New York: Revell, 1983), 559.
3. Gerald H. Anderson, ed., *Biographical Dictionary of Christian Missions* (Grand Rapids, MI: Eerdmans, 1999), 535.
4. John MacArthur, *The MacArthur New Testament Commentary: Romans 9–16* (Chicago: Moody, 1994), 83.
5. John R. W. Stott, *The Message of Romans: God's Good News for the World* (Downers Grove, IL: InterVarsity, 2001), 286.

CHAPTER FOUR: HISTORICAL UNDERSTANDINGS OF THE MISSIONARY CALL

1. J. Herbert Kane, *Understanding Christian Missions* (Grand Rapids, MI: Baker Book House, 1974), 41.
2. Marjorie A. Collins, *Manual for Today's Missionary: From Recruitment to Retirement* (Pasadena, CA: William Carey Library, 1986), 15.
3. George Wilson, "Christ's Call to Missionary Service," in *The Call, Qualifications, and Preparation of Candidates for Foreign Missionary Service*, ed. Fennell P. Turner (New York: Student Volunteer Movement for Foreign Missions, 1901), 7.
4. Elisabeth Elliot, *Shadow of the Almighty: The Life & Testament of Jim Elliot* (San Francisco: Harper & Brothers, 1958), 54.
5. Stephen Neill, *Call to Mission* (Philadelphia: Fortress, 1970), 22.
6. Elliot, *Shadow of the Almighty: The Life & Testament of Jim Elliot*, 150.
7. Robert E. Speer, *What Constitutes a Missionary Call?* (New York: Student Volunteer Movement for Foreign Missions, 1923), 12.

8. Ibid., 7.

9. Ibid., 10.

10. Robert E. Speer, "What Essentially Constitutes a Missionary Call?" in *The Call, Qualifications, and Preparation of Candidates for Foreign Missionary Service*, ed. Fennell P. Turner (New York: Student Volunteer Movement for Foreign Missions, 1901), 4–5.

11. Ibid., 6.

12. Thomas Hale, *On Being a Missionary* (Pasadena: CA: William Carey Library, 1995), 16.

13. Kenneth Scott Latourette, *The Thousand Years of Uncertainty* (Grand Rapids, MI: Zondervan, 1970), 115.

14. Ibid., 9.

15. David J. Hesselgrave, *Paradigms in Conflict: 10 Key Questions in Christian Missions Today* (Grand Rapids, MI: Kregel, 2005), 209.

16. Justice Anderson, "The Great Century and Beyond," in *Missiology: An Introduction to the Foundations, History, and Strategies of World Missions*, eds. John Mark Terry, Ebbie Smith, and Justice Anderson (Nashville, TN: Broadman and Holman, 1998), 199–218.

17. Ruth and Vishal Mangalwadi, "Who (Really) Was William Carey?" in *Perspectives on the World Christian Movement: A Reader, 3rd ed.*, eds. Ralph D. Winter and Steven C. Hawthorne (Pasadena, CA: William Carey Library, 1999), 527.

18. The categorization of significant individuals, eras, and transitions in modern missions was best captured by Ralph D. Winter in "Four Men, Three Eras, Two Transitions: Modern Missions," in *Perspectives on the World Christian Movement*, eds. Ralph D. Winter and Steven C. Hawthorne (Pasadena, CA: William Carey Library, 1999), 253–61.

19. Howard Taylor, *Hudson Taylor's Spiritual Secret* (Chicago: Moody, 1955), 120.

20. Paul G. Hiebert, *Anthropological Reflections on Missiological Issues* (Grand Rapids, MI: Baker Academic, 1994), 83.

21. Ralph D. Winter, "The Highest Priority: Cross Cultural Evangelism," in *Let the Earth Hear His Voice: Official Reference Volume, Papers and Responses*, ed. J. D. Douglas (Minneapolis, MN: World Wide Publications, 1975), 226–41.

22. Hesselgrave, *Paradigms in Conflict: 10 Key Questions in Christian Missions Today*, 231.

23. Alan Walker, *A Ringing Call to Mission* (New York: Abingdon, 1966), 31.

24. Ibid., 17.

25. Winter, *Perspectives on the World Christian Movement*, 259.

26. Urbana, "The Urbana Heritage,"
http://www.urbana.org/_articles.cfm?RecordId=60.

27. Baptist Press, "Passion Officials to Hold World Tour in '08,"
http://www.bpnews.net/bpnews.asp?ID=24715.

28. Perspectives, "About Perspectives,"
http://www.perspectives.org/site/c.eqLLIOOFKrF/b.2817899/k.C5
42/About_Perspectives.htm.

29. David Howard, "If I Could Live My Career Over Again: Reflections of
a Veteran Missionary," *Evangelical Missions Quarterly*, October 2003: 474.

30. IMB, *Exploring Your Personal Call* (International Mission Board).

31. Oswald Chambers, *My Utmost for His Highest* (Uhrichsville, OH: Discovery
House, 1992), Sept 29.

CHAPTER FIVE: HOW SPECIFIC DOES THE CALL HAVE TO BE?

1. Samuel Ling, "Toward a Biblical Doctrine of God's Call to the Ministry," China Horizon,
http://www.chinahorizon.org/Articles/031099DoctrineOfCallToMin
istry.doc.

2. Elisabeth Elliot frequently used this phrase when speaking at conferences. The validity and source of the comment was verified by the author
with Ms. Elliot.

3. R. C. Sproul, *Truths We Confess: A Layman's Guide to the Westminster Confession of
Faith, Volume 1* (Phillipsburg, NJ: P&R Publishing, 2006), 62.

CHAPTER SIX: TIMING AND THE MISSIONARY CALL

1. A. Scott Moreau and Gary R. Corwin, *Introducing World Missions: A Biblical,
Historical, and Practical Survey* (Grand Rapids, MI: Baker, 2004), 170.

2. A. T. Houghton, *Preparing to Be a Missionary* (Chicago: InterVarsity, 1956),
95.

3. Robertson McQuilken, *The Great Omission* (Grand Rapids, MI: Baker
Books, 1984), 80.

4. Robert L. Gallagher, "Spirit-Guided Mission," *Evangelical Missions Quarterly*,
July 2006: 340.

5. Robert Coote, "Good News, Bad News: North American Protestant
Overseas Personnel Statistics in Twenty-Five-Year Perspective," *International Bulletin of Missionary Research* 19, no. 6 (January 1995): 6.

6. Louis R. Cobbs, "The Missionary's Call and Training for Foreign Missions," *Baptist History and Heritage* 29, no. 4 (October 1994): 29.

7. Henry H. Jessup, "Who Ought not to Go as Foreign Missionaries," in *The Call, Qualifications, and Preparation of Candidates for Foreign Missionary Service*, ed. Fennell P. Turner (New York: Student Volunteer Movement for Foreign Missions, 1901), 20.

8. Oswald Chambers, *My Utmost for His Highest* (Uhrichsville, OH: Discovery House, 1992), 61.

9. Protestant missionaries began working among Highland Quichuas in 1902 with very little fruit. In fact, after fifty years of working among the Highland Quichuas of Chimborazo province in central Ecuador, Gospel Missionary Union missionary Julia Woodward Anderson could count on one hand the number of converts she had seen. That was 1953, and it would be two more years before the first baptism among them would occur. See John Maust, *New Song in the Andes* (Pasadena, CA: William Carey Library, 1992).

10. Elisabeth Elliot, *Through Gates of Splendor* (Carol Stream: Tyndale, 1981), 8.

11. Don W. Hillis, *I Don't Feel Called* (Wheaton, IL: Tyndale, 1973), 102.

12. Robert Murray M'Cheyne, *Memoir and Remains of the Rev. Robert Murray M'Cheyne* (London: William Middleton, 1846), 160.

13. Ibid., 243.

14. Aiden W. Tozer, *Man: The Dwelling Place of God* (Harrisburg, PA: Wingspread Publishers, 1996), 40.

15. Charles Haddon Spurgeon, *Lectures to My Students: Complete & Unabridged* (Grand Rapids, MI: Zondervan, 1977), 9.

16. Let's Go Staff, *Let's Go: New York City on a Budget* (Cambridge, MA: St. Martin's, 2006), 1.

17. Beth Greenfield, Robert Reid, and Ginger Otis, *New York City* (New York: Lonely Planet, 2004), 21.

18. The North American Mission Board and International Mission Board have partnered to form the North American People Groups Project (http://www.peoplegroups.info). This database compiles information from U.S. Census reports as well as external research, reporting statistics on nationality, languages spoken at home, ancestry, race, and people groups for cities in the United States. As of October 13, 2007, a search of the North American People Groups Project reports that 277 different nationalities live in the Louisville Metropolitan area and 76 languages other than English are spoken in Louisville homes. The North American Mission Board and Kentucky Baptist Convention verified that

the information collected was based upon Census Bureau statistics. It should be noted that the published Census Bureau information combines multiple nationalities together and therefore the official governmental statistics reflect a smaller number of nationalities than is reported by the North American Mission Board.

19. Robert E. Speer, *What Constitutes a Missionary Call?* (New York: Student Volunteer Movement for Foreign Missions, 1923), 16.

20. Elisabeth Elliot, *Shadow of the Almighty: The Life & Testament of Jim Elliot* (San Francisco: Harper & Brothers, 1958), 150.

CHAPTER SEVEN: WHAT SHOULD I DO IF MY SPOUSE DOES NOT FEEL CALLED?
1. Latin America Mission, "Why Both Partners in a Marriage Must Be Missionaries in the LAM."

CHAPTER EIGHT: GETTING TO THE FIELD
1. Marjorie A. Collins, *Manual for Today's Missionary: From Recruitment to Retirement* (Pasadena, CA: William Carey Library, 1986), 3.

2. C. Gordon Olson, *What in the World Is God Doing? The Essentials of Global Missions* (Cedar Knolls, NJ: Global Gospel Publishers, 1988), 77.

3. Don W. Hillis, *I Don't Feel Called* (Wheaton, IL: Tyndale, 1973), 34.

4. Ibid., 34.

5. A. T. Houghton, *Preparing to Be a Missionary* (Chicago: InterVarsity, 1956), 68.

6. Hillis, *I Don't Feel Called*, 36.

7. Louis R. Cobbs, "The Missionary's Call and Training for Foreign Missions," *Baptist History and Heritage* 29, no. 4 (October 1994): 30–31.

8. Ted Ward, "Repositioning Mission Agencies for the Twenty-First Century," *International Bulletin of Missionary Research* 23, no. 4 (October 1999): 146.

9. Cobbs, "The Missionary's Call and Training for Foreign Missions," 34.

10. Ibid.

11. Mike Barnett, "Creative Access Platforms: What Are They and Do We Need Them?," *Evangelical Missions Quarterly*, January 2005: 88.

12. Oswald Chambers, *My Utmost for His Highest* (Uhrichsville, OH: Discovery House, 1992), Sept. 24.

CHAPTER NINE: HINDRANCES TO GETTING TO THE FIELD
1. Isobel Kuhn, *Nests Above the Abyss* (Overseas Missions Fellowship, Robesonia PA: 1995), 300.

2. Stephen Neill, *Call to Mission* (Philadelphia: Fortress, 1970), 24.

3. Oswald Chambers, *My Utmost for His Highest* (Uhrichsville, OH: Discovery House, 1992), Sept. 29.

4. Elisabeth Elliot, *Shadow of the Almighty: The Life & Testament of Jim Elliot* (San Francisco: Harper & Brothers, 1958), 150.

5. For additional information on the concept of country shock, see *The Art of Crossing Cultures* by Craig Storti (Nicholas Brealey Publishers, 2001), 2.

6. Henry H. Jessup, "Who Ought Not to Go as Foreign Missionaries," in *The Call, Qualifications, and Preparation of Candidates for Foreign Missionary Service*, ed. Fennell P. Turner (New York: Student Volunteer Movement for Foreign Missions, 1901), 14.

7. Centers for Disease Control and Prevention, "Overweight and Obesity," http://www.cdc.gov/nccdphp/dnpa/obesity/index.htm.

8. David Mays, "Six Challenges for the Church in Missions," *Evangelical Missions Quarterly*, July 2006: 315.

9. C. S. Lewis, *The Screwtape Letters* (New York: Harper, 2001), 161.

10. Elisabeth Elliot, *The Savage My Kinsman* (Ann Arbor, MI: Servant Publishers, 1961), 63.

11. George Murray, "Missionaries' Temptations," *Evangelical Missions Quarterly*, January 1998: 67.

12. Ibid., 68.

13. A. T. Houghton, *Preparing to Be a Missionary* (Chicago: InterVarsity Press, 1956), 38.

14. Alden A. Gannett, "The Missionary Call: What Saith the Scriptures," *Bibliotheca Sacra* 117, no. 465 (January/March 1960): 37.

15. Chambers, *My Utmost for His Highest*, Sept. 30.

16. National Center for Education Statistics, "Fast Facts: 2006," http://nces.ed.gov/fastfacts/display.asp?id=31.

17. See "Living to Prove He is More Precious Than Life" in John Piper, *Don't Waste Your Life* (Wheaton, IL: Crossway Books, 2003), 107–130.

18. Chambers, *My Utmost for His Highest*, Sept. 25.

19. "Huaorani" is the accurate name of the people group formerly known as Auca. When Jim Elliot, Nate Saint, Pete Fleming, Ed McCulley, and Roger Youderian sought to reach the Huaroani people for Christ, they knew them only by the name given to them by the Quichua people, "Aucas." It was not until Elisabeth Elliot and Rachel Saint began to work among the people that they identified themselves as "Huaorani." "Auca" is actually a derogatory term as it translates as "savages" in the local Quichua dialect.

20. Elisabeth Elliot, *These Strange Ashes* (New York: Harper & Row, 1975), 70.

21. Ibid., 76.

CHAPTER TEN: CHALLENGES ON THE FIELD

1. Sherwood G. Lingenfelter and Marvin K. Mayers, *Ministering Cross-Culturally* (Grand Rapids, MI: Baker Academic, 2003), 88–89.
2. Personal blog of David and Billie Blessing, missionaries in Africa.
3. Paul Hiebert, *Anthropological Insights for Missionaries* (Grand Rapids, MI: Bauer, 1985), 68–69.
4. Elisabeth Elliot, *Shadow of the Almighty: The Life & Testament of Jim Elliot* (San Francisco: Harper & Brothers, 1958), 190.
5. Jim Elliot, *The Journals of Jim Elliot*, ed. Elisabeth Elliot (Grand Rapids, MI: Revell, 2002), 402.
6. Elisabeth Elliot, *The Savage My Kinsman* (Ann Arbor, MI: Servant, 1961), 73–75.
7. Mike Wakely, "Shadows of Doubt," *Evangelical Missions Quarterly*, October 2003: 468.

CHAPTER ELEVEN: MISSIONARY HEROES AND THE MISSIONARY CALL

1. S. N. Fitkin, *Grace Much More Abounding* (Kansas City, MO: Nazarene Publishing House, n.d.), 10–11.
2. Janet Benge and Geoff Benge, *Rachel Saint: A Star in the Jungle* (Seattle: YWAM Publishing, 2005), 29.
3. Thomas Hale, *On Being a Missionary* (Pasadena, CA: William Carey Library, 1995), 19.
4. Ibid., 16.
5. Lindsey Terry and Marilyn Terry, *Never Quit! 1,000 Sources of Strength from God's Word* (Murfreesboro, TN: Sword of the Lord, 2005), 104.
6. InterHope, "100 Quotes from World-Minded Christians of Renown," http://www.interhope.org/quotes.php.
7. Salvation Army, *All the World* (London: Oxford University, 1884), 2.
8. Norman Grubb, *C. T. Studd: Cricketer and Pioneer* (Ft. Washington, PA: Christian Literature Crusade, 1933), 132.
9. Janet Benge and Geoff Benge, *C. T. Studd: No Retreat* (Seattle: YWAM Publishing, 2005), 108.
10. Louis R. Cobbs, "The Missionary's Call and Training for Foreign Missions," *Baptist History and Heritage* 29, no. 4 (October 1994): 29.
11. James Gilmour, *James Gilmour of Mongolia: His Diaries, Letters and Reports*, ed. Richard Lovett (Boston: Elibron Classics, 2001), 42–43.
12. C. Gordon Olson, *What in the World Is God Doing? The Essentials of Global Missions* (Cedar Knolls, NJ: Global Gospel Publishers, 1988), 86.
13. Wayne Vleck, *Dakota Martyrs: The Story You Never Heard* (Valley City, ND: Bunyan Family Books, 2004), 82.

14. Hale, *On Being a Missionary*, 17.
15. For source information as well as additional details about the life and ministry of David Brainerd, see Jonathan Edwards, *David Brainerd: His Life and Diary* (Chicago: Moody, 1949).
16. Jonathan Edwards, *David Brainerd: His Life and Diary* (Chicago: Moody, 1949), 158–159.
17. For source information as well as additional details about the life and ministry of William Carey, see F. Deaville Walker, *William Carey: Missionary Pioneer and Statesman* (Chicago: Moody, 1951) and Timothy F. George, *Faithful Witness: The Life & Mission of William Carey* (Birmingham, AL: New Hope, 1991).
18. George Smith, *The Life of William Carey: Shoemaker & Missionary* (New York: J. M. Dent & Sons, Ltd., 1913), 29.
19. Mary Drewery, *William Carey: A Biography* (Grand Rapids, MI: Zondervan, 1978), 35.
20. For source information as well as additional details about the life and ministry of John Paton, see J. Theodore Mueller, *John G. Paton: Missionary to the New Hebrides 1824–1907* (Grand Rapids, MI: Zondervan, 1941).
21. J. Theodore Mueller, *John G. Paton: Missionary to the New Hebrides 1824–1907* (Grand Rapids, MI: Zondervan, 1941), 29.
22. Ibid., 31.
23. Ibid., 32.
24. For source information as well as additional details about the life and ministry of J. Hudson Taylor, see Howard Taylor, *Hudson Taylor and the China Inland Mission: The Growth of a Work of God* (China Inland Mission, 1919) and Howard Taylor and Mary G. Taylor, *Hudson Taylor's Spiritual Secret* (Chicago: Moody, 1954).
25. Dr. and Mrs. Howard Taylor, *Biography of James Hudson Taylor* (Robesonia, PA: Overseas Missions Fellowship, 1973), 15.
26. Daniel Bacon, "How Hudson Taylor Got Recruits for China," *Evangelical Missions Quarterly*, July 1984: 231.
27. Taylor, *Biography of James Hudson Taylor*, 23.
28. Howard Taylor, *Hudson Taylor and the China Inland Mission: The Growth of a Work of God* (China Inland Mission, 1919), 8.
29. Joseph Williams, *You're on a Mission: A 31-Day Devotional Journey Around the World* (Indianapolis, IN: Dog Ear Publishing, 2007), 9.
30. For source information as well as additional details about the life and ministry of Charlotte "Lottie" Digges Moon, see Keith Harper, ed., *Send the Light: Lottie Moon's Letters and Other Writings* (Macon, GA: Mercer University Press, 2002); Catherine B. Allen, *The New Lottie Moon Story* (Nashville:

Broadman, 1980); and Southern Baptist Historical Library and Archives Bibliographies, "Lottie Moon," http://www.sbhla.org/bio_moon.htm.

31. Wyatt M. Rogers, *Christianity and Womanhood: Evolving Roles and Responsibilities* (Westport, CT: Praeger/Greenwood, 2002), 76.

32. Catherine B. Allen, *The New Lottie Moon Story* (Nashville, TN: Broadman, 1980), 275.

33. For source information as well as additional details about the life and ministry of Amy Carmichael, see Elisabeth Elliot, *A Chance to Die: The Life and Legacy of Amy Carmichael* (Old Tappan, NJ: Revell, 1987) and Frank Houghton, *Amy Carmichael of Dohnavur: The Story of a Lover and Her Beloved* (Ft. Washington, PA: Christian Literature Crusade, 1953).

34. Frank Houghton, *Amy Carmichael of Dohnavur: The Story of a Lover and Her Beloved* (Ft. Washington, PA: Christian Literature Crusade, 1954), 45.

35. Elisabeth Elliot, *A Chance to Die: The Life and Legacy of Amy Carmichael* (Old Tappan, NJ: Revell, 1987), 176.

36. Lois Hoadley Dick, *Amy Carmichael: Let the Little Children Come* (Chicago: Moody, 1984), 33.

37. For source information as well as additional details about the life and ministry of Cam Townsend, see James C. Hefley and Marti Hefley, *Uncle Cam: The Story of William Cameron Townsend, Founder of the Wycliffe Bible Translators and the Summer Institute of Linguistics* (Waco, TX: Word Books, 1974).

38. James C. Hefley and Marti Hefley, *Uncle Cam: The Story of William Cameron Townsend, Founder of the Wycliffe Bible Translators and the Summer Institute of Linguistics* (Waco, TX: Word Books, 1974), 23.

39. Ibid.

40. For source information as well as additional details about the life and ministry of Jim Elliot, see Elisabeth Elliot, *Shadow of the Almighty: The Life & Testament of Jim Elliot* (New York: HarperOne, 1989); Elisabeth Elliot, *Through Gates of Splendor* (Carol Stream, IL: Tyndale House, 1986); and Jim Elliot, *The Journals of Jim Elliot*, ed. Elisabeth Elliot (New York: Revell, 2002).

41. Elisabeth Elliot, *Shadow of the Almighty: The Life & Testament of Jim Elliot* (San Francisco: Harper & Brothers, 1958), 45.

42. Ibid., 236.

CHAPTER TWELVE: UNDERSTANDING AND ANSWERING THE MISSIONARY CALL

1. J. Herbert Kane, *The Making of a Missionary* (Grand Rapids, MI: Baker Book House, 1979), 46–49.

2. Charles Kellogg, *Charless Kellogg The Nature Singer: His Book* (White Fish, MT: Kessinger Publications, 2004), 141–143.

BIBLIOGRAPHY

Aeschliman, Gordon Peterson. *Maximum Impact Short-Term Mission: The God-Commanded, Repetitive Deployment of Swift, Temporary, Non-Professional Missionaries.* Minneapolis, MN: STEM Press, 2003.

Allen, Catherine B. *The New Lottie Moon Story.* Nashville: Broadman, 1980.

Allen, Madalyn Elizabeth Burtoft. "Call to Missions: A Historical and Psychological Understanding of the Christian Construct in the Context of Psychological Assessment." Ph.D. Diss., Department of Psychology, Fuller Theological Seminary, 2001.

Anderson, Gerald H., ed. *Biographical Dictionary of Christian Missions.* Grand Rapids, MI: Eerdmans, 1999.

Anderson, Gerald H., Robert T. Coote, Norman A. Horner, and James M. Phillips. *Mission Legacies: Biographical Studies of Leaders of the Modern Missionary Movement.* Maryknoll, NY: Orbis Books, 1995.

Anderson, Justice. "The Great Century and Beyond." In *Missiology: An Introduction to the Foundations, History, and Stategies of World Missions,* edited by John Mark Terry, Ebbie Smith, and Justice Anderson, 199–218. Nashville, TN: Broadman and Holman, 1998.

Bacon, Daniel. "How Hudson Taylor Got Recruits for China." *Evangelical Missions Quarterly*, July 1984: 226–31.

Barnett, Mike. "Creative Access Platforms: What Are They and Do We Need Them?" *Evangelical Missions Quarterly*, January 2005: 88–96.

Benge, Janet and Geoff Benge. *C. T. Studd: No Retreat*. Seattle: YWAM Publishing, 2005.

—————. *Rachel Saint: A Star in the Jungle*. Seattle: YWAM Publishing, 2005.

Blackaby, Henry T. *Experiencing God*. Nashville, TN: Broadman and Holman, 2004.

Bogosian, Phil. "The Time Has Not Yet Come: Why America is Experiencing Judgment." *Mission Frontiers*, March/April 1992: 3–4.

Butler, Philip. "Is There a New Way Forward?" In *Kingdom Partnerships for Synergy in Missions*, edited by William D. Taylor, 9–30. Pasadena, CA: William Covey, 1994.

Carver, William Owen. *Missions in the Plan of the Ages*. Nashville, TN: Broadman Press, 1951.

Chamberlain, Jacob. "The Call to Foreign Missionary Work." In *The Call, Qualifications, and Preparation of Candidates for Foreign Missionary Service*, edited by Fennell P. Turner, 10–13. New York: Student Volunteer Movement for Foreign Missions, 1901.

Chambers, Oswald. *My Utmost for His Highest*. Uhrichsville, OH: Discovery House, 1992.

Cobbs, Louis R. "The Missionary's Call and Training for Foreign Missions." *Baptist History and Heritage* 29, no. 4 (October 1994): 26–36.

Collins, Marjorie A. *Manual for Today's Missionary: From Recruitment to Retirement*. Pasadena, CA: William Carey Library, 1986.

Coote, Robert. "Good News, Bad News: North American Protestant Overseas Personnel Statistics in Twenty-Five-Year

Perspective." *International Bulletin of Missionary Research* 19, no. 6 (January 1995): 6–13.

Decker, Murray. "The Emerging College Generation and Missions: Issues, Attitudes, Postures, and Passions." *Evangelical Missions Quarterly*, July 2007.

Dick, Lois Hoadley. *Amy Carmichael: Let the Little Children Come.* Chicago: Moody, 1984.

Drewery, Mary. *William Carey: A Biography.* Grand Rapids, MI: Zondervan, 1978.

Edwards, Jonathan. *David Brainerd, His Life and Diary.* Chicago: Moody, 1949.

Elliot, Elisabeth. *A Chance to Die: The Life and Legacy of Amy Carmichael.* Old Tappan, NJ: Revell, 1987.

_____. *The Savage My Kinsman.* Ann Arbor, MI: Servant Publishers, 1961.

_____. *Shadow of the Almighty: The Life & Testament of Jim Elliot.* San Francisco: Harper & Brothers, 1958.

_____. *A Slow and Certain Light.* Waco, TX: Word Books, 1975.

_____. *These Strange Ashes.* New York: Harper & Row, 1975.

_____. *Through Gates of Splendor.* Carol Stream, IL: Tyndale, 1981.

Elliot, Jim. *The Journals of Jim Elliot.* Edited by Elisabeth Elliot. Grand Rapids, MI: Revell, 2002.

Fitkin, S. N. *Grace Much More Abounding.* Kansas City, MO: Nazarene Publishing House, n.d.

Fuller, Lois K. *Going to the Nations: An Introduction to Cross-Cultural Missions.* ACTS, 2001.

Gallagher, Robert L. "Spirit-Guided Mission." *Evangelical Missions Quarterly*, July 2006: 336–341.

Gannett, Alden A. "The Missionary Call: What Saith the Scriptures." *Bibliotheca Sacra* 117, no. 465 (January/March 1960): 32–40.

George, Timothy. *Faithful Witness: The Life & Mission of William Carey.* Birmingham, AL: New Hope, 1991.

Gilmour, James. *James Gilmour of Mongolia: His Diaries, Letters and Reports.* Edited by Richard Lovett. Boston: Elibron Classics, 2001.

Goff, William E. "Missionary Call and Service." In *Missiology: An Introduction to the Foundations, History, and Strategies of World Missions,* edited by John Mark Terry, Ebbie Smith, and Justice Anderson, 334–346. Nashville, TN: Broadman and Holman, 1998.

Greenfield, Beth and Robert Reid. *New York City.* New York: Lonely Planet, 2004.

Grubb, Norman. *C. T. Studd: Cricketer and Pioneer.* Ft. Washington, PA: Christian Literature Crusade, 1933.

Hale, Thomas. *On Being a Missionary.* Pasadena, CA: William Carey Library, 1995.

Hefley, James C. and Marti Hefley. *Uncle Cam: The Story of William Cameron Townsend, Founder of the Wycliffe Bible Translators and the Summer Institute of Linguistics.* Waco, TX: Word Books, 1974.

Henry, Matthew. *Matthew Henry's Commentary on the Whole Bible: Acts–Revelation.* New York: Revell, 1983.

Hesselgrave, David J. *Paradigms in Conflict: 10 Key Questions in Christian Missions Today.* Grand Rapids, MI: Kregel, 2005.

Hiebert, Paul. *Anthropological Reflections on Missiological Issues.* Grand Rapids, MI: Baker Academic, 1994.

_____. *Anthropological Insights for Missionaries.* Grand Rapids, MI: Baker, 1985.

Hillis, Don W. *I Don't Feel Called.* Wheaton, IL: Tyndale, 1973.

Houghton, A. T. *Preparing to Be a Missionary.* Chicago: InterVarsity Press, 1956.

Houghton, Frank. *Amy Carmichael of Dohnavur: The Story of a Lover and Her Beloved.* Ft. Washington, PA: Christian Literature Crusade, 1953.

Howard, David. "If I Could Live My Career Over Again: Reflections of a Veteran Missionary." *Evangelical Missions Quarterly,* October 2003: 474–78.

_____. *What Makes a Missionary.* Chicago: Moody, 1987.

Howard, Kevin L. "A Call to Missions: Is There Such a Thing?" *Evangelical Missions Quarterly,* October 2003: 462–65.

Hulse, Erroll. *Adoniram Judson and the Missionary Call.* Reformation Today Trust, 1996.

International Mission Board. *Exploring Your Personal Call.* International Mission Board.

Jessup, Henry H. "Who Ought not to Go as Foreign Missionaries." In *The Call, Qualifications, and Preparation of Candidates for Foreign Missionary Service,* edited by Fennell P. Turner, 14–22. New York: Student Volunteer Movement for Foreign Missions, 1901.

Kane, J. Herbert. *The Making of a Missionary.* Grand Rapids, MI: Baker Book House, 1975.

_____. *Understanding Christian Missions.* Grand Rapids, MI: Baker Book House, 1974.

Kellogg, Charles. *Charles Kellogg the Nature Singer: His Book.* White Fish, MT: Kessinger Publications, 2004.

Kuhn, Isobel. *Nests Above the Abyss.* Overseas Missions Fellowship, Robesonia, PA: 1995.

Latourette, Kenneth Scott. *The First Five Centuries.* Grand Rapids, MI: Zondervan, 1970.

_____. *The Thousand Years of Uncertainty.* Grand Rapids, MI: Zondervan, 1970.

Let's Go Staff. *Let's Go: New York City on a Budget.* Cambridge, MA: St. Martin's Press, 2006.

Lewis, C. S. *The Screwtape Letters.* New York, Harper, 2001.

Lingenfelter, Sherwood G. and Marvin K. Mayers. *Ministering Cross-Culturally.* Grand Rapids, MI: Baker Academic, 2003.

MacArthur, John. *The MacArthur New Testament Commentary: Romans 9–16.* Chicago: Moody Publishers, 1994.

Mangalwadi, Ruth and Vishal Mangalwadi. "Who (Really) Was William Carey?" In *Perspectives on the World Christian Movement: A Reader, 3rd ed.,* edited by Ralph D. Winter and Steven C. Hawthorne, 525–528. Pasadena, CA: William Carey Library, 1999.

Maust, John. *New Song in the Andes.* Pasadena, CA: William Carey Library, 1992.

Mays, David. "Six Challenges for the Church in Missions." *Evangelical Missions Quarterly,* July 2006: 304–15.

McConaughy, David. *The World-Call to Men of Today.* New York: The Board of Foreign Missions of the PCUSA, 1908.

McConnell, Walter. "The Missionary Call: A Biblical and Practical Appraisal." *Evangelical Missions Quarterly,* April 2007: 210–17.

M'Cheyne, Robert Murray. *Memoir and Remains of the Rev. Robert Murray M'Cheyne.* London: Willam Middleton, 1846.

McQuilken, Robertson. *The Great Omission.* Grand Rapids, MI: Baker Books, 1984.

Milton, Owen. *Christian Missionaries.* Bryntirion, U.K.: Bryntirion Press, 1995.

Moon, Lottie. *Send the Light: Lottie Moon's Letters and Other Writings,* edited by Keith Harper. Macon, GA: Mercer University Press, 2002.

Moreau, A. Scott and Gary R. Corwin. *Introducing World Missions: A Biblical, Historical, and Practical Survey*. Grand Rapids, MI: Baker, 2004.

Mueller, J. Theodore. *John G. Paton*. Grand Rapids, MI: Zondervan, 1941.

Murray, George. "Missionaries' Temptations." *Evangelical Missions Quarterly*, January 1998: 66–68.

Nault, Jennifer. *Georgia*. New York: Weigl, 2002.

Neill, Stephen. *Call to Mission*. Philadelphia: Fortress Press, 1970.

Olson, C. Gordon. *What in the World Is God Doing? The Essentials of Global Missions*. Cedar Knolls, NJ: Global Gospel Publishers, 1988.

Packer, J. I. *Knowing God*. Downers Grove, IL: InterVarsity, 1993.

Paton, John G. *Missionary Patriarch: The True Story of John G. Paton*. Men of Courage. San Antonio, TX: Vision Forum, 2001.

Piper, John. *Don't Waste Your Life*. Wheaton, IL: Crossway Books, 2003.

_____. *Let the Nations Be Glad!* Grand Rapids, MI: Baker Books, 1993.

Reapsome, Jim. "What Happened to the Uttermost Parts." *Evangelical Missions Quarterly*, January 1999: 6–7.

Robbins, Joseph C. *The Appeal of Foreign Missions to Young Life*. Boston: American Baptist Foreign Mission Society, 1917.

Rogers, Wyatt M. *Christianity and Womanhood: Evolving Roles and Responsibilities*. Westport, CT: Praeger/Greenwood, 2002.

Rupert, Marybeth. *The Emergence of the Independent Missionary Agency as an American Institution 1860–1917*. Ann Arbor, MI: University Microfilms International, 1974.

Rusten, E. Michael and Sharon O. Rusten. *The Complete Book of When and Where: In the Bible and Throughout History*. Carol Stream, IL: Tyndale House, 2005.

Salvation Army. *All the World*. London: Oxford University, 1884.

Sargent, Douglas N. *The Making of a Missionary*. London: Hodder and Stoughton, 1960.

Shibley, David. *A Force in the Earth: The Charismatic Renewal and World Evangelism*. Lake Mary, FL: Creation House, 1989.

Smith, George. *The Life of William Carey: Shoemaker & Missionary*. New York: J. M. Dent & Sons, Ltd., 1913.

Speer, Robert E. *What Constitutes a Missionary Call?* New York: Student Volunteer Movement for Foreign Missions, 1923.

_____. "What Essentially Constitutes a Missionary Call?" In *The Call, Qualifications, and Preparation of Candidates for Foreign Missionary Service*, edited by Fennell P. Turner, 3–6. New York: Student Volunteer Movement for Foreign Missions, 1901.

Sproul, R. C. *Truths We Confess: A Layman's Guide to the Westminster Confession of Faith. Vol. 1*. Phillipsburg, NJ: P & R, 2006.

Spurgeon, Charles Haddon. *Lectures to My Students: Complete & Unabridged*. Grand Rapids, MI: Zondervan, 1977.

Storti, Craig. *The Art of Crossing Cultures*. Boston: Nicholas Brealey Publishers, 2001.

Stott, John R. W. *The Message of Romans: God's Good News for the World*. Downers Grove, IL: InterVarsity Press, 2001.

Taylor, Dr. and Mrs. Howard. *Biography of James Hudson Taylor*. Robesonia, PA: Overseas Missions Fellowship, 1973.

Taylor, Howard. *Hudson Taylor and China Inland Mission: The Growth of a Work of God*. China Inland Mission, 1919.

_____. *Hudson Taylor's Spiritual Secret*. Chicago: Moody, 1954.

Terry, Lindsey and Marilyn Terry. *Never Quit! 1,000 Sources of Strength from God's Word*. Murfreesboro, TN: Sword of the Lord, 2005.

Tozer, Aiden W. *Man: The Dwelling Place of God.* Harrisburg, PA: Wingspread Publishers, 1996.

Turner, Fennell P., ed. *The Call, Qualifications, and Preparation of Candidates for Foreign Missionary Service.* New York: Student Volunteer Movement for Foreign Missions, 1901.

Twain, Mark. *The Innocents Abroad.* Leipzig: Bernhard Tauchnitz, 1879.

Vleck, Wayne. *Dakota Martyrs: The Story You Never Heard.* Valley City, ND: Bunyan Family Books, 2004.

Wagner, C. Peter. "My Pilgrimage in Mission." *International Bulletin of Missionary Research* 23, no. 4 (October 1999): 164–67.

Wakely, Mike. "Shadows of Doubt." *Evangelical Missions Quarterly,* October 2003: 468–72.

Walker, Alan. *A Ringing Call to Mission.* New York: Abingdon Press, 1966.

Walker, F. Deaville. *William Carey: Missionary Pioneer and Statesman.* Chicago: Moody, 1951.

Waltke, Bruce. *Finding the Will of God: A Pagan Notion?* Gresham, OR: Vision House, 1995.

Ward, Ted. "Repositioning Mission Agencies for the Twenty-First Century." *International Bulletin of Missionary Research* 23, no. 4 (October 1999): 146–53.

Williams, Joseph. *You're on a Mission: A 31-Day Devotional Journey Around the World.* Indianapolis, IN: Dog Ear Publishing, 2007.

Wilson, George. "Christ's Call to Missionary Service." In *The Call, Qualifications, and Preparation of Candidates for Foreign Missionary Service,* edited by Fennell P. Turner, 7–9. New York: Student Volunteer Movement for Foreign Missions, 1901.

Winter, Ralph D. "Are You Finding Your Way Into God's Highest Call for You?" *Mission Frontiers,* January/February 2007: 1–5.

_____. "Four Men, Three Eras, Two Transitions: Modern Missions." In *Perspectives on the World Christian Movement*, edited by Ralph D. Winter and Steven C. Hawthorne, 253–61. Pasadena, CA: William Carey Library, 1999.

_____. "The Highest Priority: Cross Cultural Evangelism." In *Let the Earth Hear His Voice: Official Reference Volume, Papers and Responses*, edited by J. D. Douglas, 226–41. Minneapolis, MN: World Wide Publications, 1975.

_____. "Join the World Christian Movement." In *Perspectives on the World Christian Movement*, edited by Ralph D. Winter and Steven C. Hawthorne, 718–23. Pasadena, CA: William Carey Library, 1999.

Wright, Christopher J. H. *The Mission of God: Unlocking the Bible's Grand Narrative.* Downers Grove, IL: InterVarsity, 2006.

Zwemer, Samuel. "The Glory of the Impossible." In *Perspectives on the World Christian Movement*, edited by Ralph D. Winter and Steven C. Hawthorne, 311–16. Pasadena, CA: William Carey Library, 1999.

SUBJECT INDEX

SCRIPTURE INDEX

For additional missions resources visit Reaching and Teaching, Dr. David Sills' ministry website

- Downloadable Resources for Intercultural Studies
- Sermon Audio and Conference Powerpoints
- Dr. Sills' blog, Culturality & Missiology
- Dr. Sills' speaking schedule

www.ReachingAndTeaching.org